How to

A COMMON-SENSE GUIDE FOR

Survive

TURNING A DIFFICULT TIME IN

Your

BOTH YOUR LIVES INTO A LOVING,

Aging

COOPERATIVE RELATIONSHIP.

Parents

. . . so you and they can enjoy life.

Raeann Berman and
Bernard H. Shulman, M.D.

SURREY BOOKS

HOW TO SURVIVE YOUR AGING PARENTS is published by
Surrey Books, Inc., 230 E. Ohio St., Suite 120, Chicago, IL 60611.

Second edition: 1 2 3 4 5

This book is manufactured in the United States of America.

Library of Congress Cataloging-in-Publication data:
Berman, Raeann, 1932–
      How to survive your aging parents : so you and they can enjoy
   life / Raeann Berman and Bernard H. Shulman.—2nd ed.
        p. cm.
      Includes bibliography references and index.
      ISBN 1-57284-037-4 (pbk.)
       1.Aging parents—Care—Unites States. 2.Aging parents—
   United States—Psychology. 3.Adult children of aging parents
   —United States—Attitudes. I. Shulman, Bernard H. II.Title

HQ1063.6 .B473 2001
306.874—dc21   2001031137

Editorial and production: *Bookcrafters, Inc., Chicago*
Cover and book design: *Joan Sommers Design, Chicago*

For prices on quantity purchases or for free book catalog,
contact Surrey Books at the above address.

This title is distributed to the trade by Publishers Group West.

*To all generations of elders
and their children*

CONTENTS

6
Breaking Out of Old, Destructive Patterns

How to counteract manipulative behavior and power plays by understanding our parents' motives and setting our own objectives.

7
How to Help Our Parents Compensate Constructively

Helping aging parents find positive ways of making up for their losses; a review of organized programs for seniors.

8
Taking Care of Yourself As Well As Your Parent

Strategies for sharing the care of aging relatives; managing stress and guilt as care-giver.

9
When Your Parent Has to Move: How to Find the Best Living Arrangements

How to find the best housing options for your parents, whether in your home with back-up care or in independent or assisted living facilities.

10
How to Talk About Difficult Subjects

Discussing topics such as remarriage, finances, living arrangements, driver's licenses, illness, and death with the elderly.

11
Dealing with Confusion and Memory Loss

Causes of debility among the aged; symptoms to watch for; coping with malnutrition, medication, and medical care; ways to improve memory.

12
What Does the Future Hold for America's Seniors?

Changing societal attitudes and evolving social institutions for our expanding senior population.

Appendix of Resources

Organizations, associations, and programs for seniors.

ACKNOWLEDGMENTS

Many people believe in this book. We want to thank them all for their support and encouragement:

To our spouses, Sid Berman and Phyllis Shulman an, who tolerated late or missed dinners with true grace under pressure.

To Lawrence Lazurus, M.D., assistant professor of psychiatry at Rush Medical College and psychiatric consultant to the Johnston Bowman Health Center for the Elderly, Rush-Presbyterian-St. Luke's Medical Center, Chicago; Sanford Finkel, M.D., geriatric psychiatrist in Chicago; Harvey Gochros, Ph.D., University of Hawaii School of Social Work; Jean Gochros, Ph.D., psychotherapist, Honolulu, Hawaii; Margaret Huyck, Ph.D., president of Older Women's League (OWL) of Illinois and professor in the Institute of Pyschology, Illinois Institute of Technology; Carol Gaetjens,, Ph.D., lecturer at Northwestern University and former coordinator of the M.A. in Gerontology Program at Northeastern Illinois University; Mary Ann Manion, director, and Nina Afremow, social worker, at Gidwitz Place for Assisted Living, Deerfield, IL; Barbara G. Carter, director of marketing and communications for the Council for Jewish Elderly, Chicago, IL; Hazel Childs, director of family services for The WealShire, Lincolnshire, IL; Sharon Jarchin, president, Sharon Jarchin Health Care Marketing, Huntington, New York—our sincere thanks for their interest and willingness to contribute to the completion of this book.

Our grateful appreciation goes to the reviewers of the first edition of *How to Survive Your Aging Parents*. Their whole-hearted enthusiasm brought readers from all over the world.

T'hanks must also be said to our publisher, Susan Schwartz, for her belief in us and her understanding of the need for this kind of book for adult children of aging parents.

To the memory of our parents, Harry and Yetta Shulman and Saul and Hessie Goldberg. And to our children: Mark, Robert, and Cynthia and Stacey and Laurel, and all their children, who, in time, may learn how to survive their aging parents.

PREFACE

It is no longer unusual for Americans to live to be more than 90 years old. Average life expectancy today is 77.5 years. A newborn baby girl can expect to live to the average age of 79 years while baby boys can average around 74 years. For babies born at the turn of the twentieth century the odds were quite different—average length of life was about 49.5 years, again favoring the female population, with average life expectancy for baby girls running at around 51 years and 48 for baby boys.

There are 35 million people over the age of 65, and they will number 54 million by 2020. The aging of the American population is a fact of life.

The implications of this phenomenon are far-reaching but perhaps have the most profound effect on the middle-aged care-givers who become responsible for the expanding senior population: their children and relatives. These care-givers, it is estimated, range in age from 40 to 69; 72 percent of them are women. The care recipients, on the other hand, range from 65 to 105 years old, and 69 percent of them are women. It quickly becomes obvious that virtually the entire population, at one time or another, must face the special problems of aging.

The task of caring for the elderly is mostly carried on in the home by family members. Even though there are at present more than 2 million beds in long-term care facilities (which is expected to rise to 5 million over the next 20 years), two to three times that number of seniors are cared for at home. The stress, anxiety, and interpersonal problems generated by caring for a frail elder at home or in a nursing home are great. The variety of issues, problems—and, yes, rewards—are as great as the variety of people in our society.

Guidance for the middle-aged "kids" who find themselves responsible for elderly parents is long overdue. For instance, it is known through interviews of older patients and their appointed decision-makers (should they become incompetent) that views about life-extending care are rarely discussed. Indeed, in only 10 percent of the cases had the patient expressed his or her preferences in this area, and only a negligible number had signed living wills. The need for more meaningful communication between care-giver and care-recipient is apparent.

Family support systems, decent housing, good nutrition, economic stability, and the provision of health care are essential to the well-being of our seniors. These requisites are, usually, willingly provided by loving children. But even more is asked of these middle-generation care-givers. They must be able to understand and deal effectively with the emotional responses, behavior, and motives of their aging parents or relatives. Further, they must not themselves succumb to the stresses and anxieties inherent in their role as, inevitably, their charge loses ground to an irreversible condition: aging.

If you are now or will become responsible for aging parents or relatives, this book can provide essential insights to help you—and your charge— "survive" each other. That final time together can be one of love, appreciation, and mutual respect—if you are emotionally prepared to encounter it.

Christine K. Cassel, M.D.
Chairman, Department of Geriatrics and Human Development,
Mount Sinai Medical Center, New York

F O R E W O R D

Quite often there is a "problem old person" in today's American family. Equally common are middle-aged "kids" who are suffering severe anxiety and guilt about their relationship with their elderly parents. Many Americans are living longer and enjoying it less.

In Dr. Bernard Shulman's many years of practice, he has come to know the special sadness and frustration of both the elderly who feel they have outlived their usefulness and their middle-aged children who can't cope with their parents' physical, mental, and emotional problems. Award-winning writer Raeann Berman has a social-psychology background and has published widely on family problems and social issues.

We have a dichotomy in this country. On the one hand, we employ heroic measures to prolong life, to make people as comfortable and pain-free as possible. On the other, we ignore the quality of their lives. In short, we ignore their real needs—to be honored, respected, and loved, not treated like recalcitrant children. There's nothing "cute" about being old.

In the United States today there are 35 million people over the age of 65—13 percent of the population. By the year 2030, an estimated 20 percent of Americans, or around 70 million, will have passed their 65th birthday. Of the "aging population" today, 41 percent of the women and 15 percent of the men live alone; some prefer it that way, others do not. Another 83 percent of the men and 57 percent of the women reside with their children or other family members. And the rest, around 5 million, live in sheltered-care facilities and nursing homes.

People age 85 and older are the largest segment of the population in nursing homes and sheltered-care facilities. Approximately 192 people per 1,000 live in nursing and retirement homes. About three-quarters of the residents are women.

Most of these people never thought they'd live to be very old. "I never dreamed my mother [or father] would be like this," comes the cry from their children.

There's a big gap between the elderly and their middle-aged children. And we believe that gap can be bridged.

The ideas in this book grow out of the philosophy of Alfred Adler, Rudolf Dreikurs, and their students: human beings are social animals with a compelling need to belong and have a place in society. Throughout childhood and early adult life we strive to find and secure that place for ourselves. Many of the problems of elderly people arise from their losing their place in the social structure; as a result, they come to feel that their lives are meaningless, and they lose self-esteem.

Older peoples' attempts to compensate for slipping self-esteem often take the form of behavior that baffles, frustrates, and infuriates younger relatives and loved ones. The purpose of this book is to help you understand what's going on, why your parents are acting the way they are, and what you can—and cannot—do about it.

The wounds elderly people and their adult children inflict on each other can be healed. In the chapters that follow, we will show you "how to survive your aging parents," how to get over the guilt and anxiety, and how to go on to the next step—loving cooperation.

Raeann Goldberg Berman
Bernard H. Shulman, M.D., F.A.P.A.

ONE

Living on the Far Side

YOU'RE ALONE most of the time. When you do relate to people, it tends to be in terms of money. You're paying them to do something for you—bring in your dry-cleaning, pick up a quart of milk, make a phone call to the "outside." You play your television all day long so there are voices in the house. You'd like to hem your slacks or sew a button on a shirt, but you can't see well enough to thread the needle. And, besides, you can't remember where you put the sewing kit.

You cry a lot lately. You remember what it was like to be independent, young, healthy. You remember what it was like to have brothers and sisters. You remember your own mother better now—the touch of her hands, the bread she baked for special holidays. Sometimes you can't remember your daughter's married name. Or her telephone number. Sometimes you forget whether or not you had dinner last night. Sometimes you wonder why you're still alive.

Your mother called you again at work today. "When are you coming over? I'm lonely." "I was there yesterday, Mom. I can't make it till the weekend. What do you need? I'll bring it." You hang up and the headache begins. Or the stomach ache or the zinging in the back of your neck. You don't sleep well anymore. You wake up at 4 A.M. and see your mother crossing the street alone, just your mother and her cane and all the cars and trucks. And you start to worry. Every time you go there now, she cries, gives you hurt looks. Or asks you what you're planning to do with your extra bedroom now that Ellen is married and Jimmy has his own place. You're losing your sense of humor. You're starting to feel old.

Staring Across the Generation Gap

The distance between us and our aging parents seems insurmountable. We're at two different places on life's journey, struggling with a vision of our own mortality, wondering why we wake up hurting all over now, looking in the mirror sometimes and seeing a tired face and hair that has the effrontery to turn gray. We've raised our kids, gone through the fire of their adolescence. And we've paid our dues in the workplace. Now we want to relax, have fun, do the things we've postponed.

The vision of our mortality both depresses us and spray paints "Live now. It's my turn" on our consciousness. The more adventurous of us pay attention to the graffiti. We decide to take more vacations. Or to work less. Or to enroll in courses in Egyptology or scuba diving. We deserve it!

But while our thrust is to make the most of the life we have left, our elderly parents are experiencing loss and failure on almost every front. All too often, they take it out on their children. Consider the case of the Harrington family.

Tim and Barbara Harrington have reservations for Bangkok. Tim stopped there briefly on his way home from Vietnam during the closing days of the war, and he promised himself he'd see those gorgeous temples and visit a Thai marketplace once the war was over. The Harringtons go to visit his mother, Mabel, age 80, who lives alone in a senior high-rise building. This is how the visit goes.

"Ma, we're leaving tomorrow. Be on vacation for two weeks. Don't forget: call cousin Buddy if you have problems."

"Why should I have problems!" Mabel retorts. "I live here alone all the time. I manage fine without you both, thank you."

"What's wrong, Ma? What did we do?" Tim is bewildered. Isn't Ma happy that he's realizing his dream?

"Nothing. Nothing." His mother begins to sob. "Just go on about your business, and don't worry about me."

Tim and Barbara slink out of the apartment, chastened, guilty, low in spirits. Tim says, "I feel like a six-year-old who robbed the cookie jar. But I still don't know what's bugging her."

Barbara mutters between her teeth. "Well, she won again. Ruined our trip. And you'll be worrying every minute we're gone."

What's really happening here?

At first glance Tim's mother is one of those indomitable old ladies we see so often on television—cookie-cutter old lady. Strong-willed and independent, she never has asked anyone for anything in her entire life. If this were a TV world, she'd continue until one night she simply closed her eyes and died, thereby relieving her children of responsibility for her future.

Understanding Our Parents' Losses

In real life, Mrs. Harrington is experiencing a sense of loss and failure in three critical areas of her life: sexual, occupational, and social.

For most very old people, particularly widows and widowers, the joys of sexual life are over. There is no sharing of love, no mutual pleasing of two partners, no fights to make up. Usually the partner is gone, taking with him or her the history of shared pleasure. So the surviving spouse has lost her or his function as a sexual being.

However, sex does not cease to be a powerful force in our lives when child-bearing stops. There is no cut-off of feelings when the hormones retreat. The need for closeness and touching is still there. Many long-lived elderly, for whom that segment of life is "functionally" over, feel a deep sense of loss. Mrs. Harrington misses Mr. Harrington.

Secondly, Mrs. Harrington feels "non-contributory." In our culture, where the old are frequently isolated from the working world, not allowed to give of themselves according to their abilities, the loss of occupation is experienced as a loss of self. Mrs. Harrington, like many women of her generation, was a care-giver. She never worked outside the home, but she functioned at the peak of her powers in homemaking, cooking, and pitching in to help others. In her more bitter moments, she wonders why it is that she, a care-giver, a sacrificer her whole life, should now be alone with no one seeing to her comfort.

The Role Gives Us a Script

Who we are and what we stand for determine our role in the world. Our personal identity, our uniqueness, depends to a great extent upon the functions we perform—the role we play.

Mrs. Harrington knew her role and functioned within its structure to systematize her time and energy. When she got up in the morning, she prepared for the demands of the day. But now she's elderly and can't fulfill that role, and she keenly feels its loss.

She's no longer "working" as she once did. She can't do the heavy cleaning or carry bundles home from the market. It hurts her to see her job disappear. Her sense of uselessness is intensified when she sees Tim and Barbara so busy in their lives. "Flying around all the time" she calls it.

Mrs. Harrington is also experiencing significant losses as a social being: her friends are dead or dying off, she lacks the opportunity to meet new people, and she feels so diminished that she's sure she's not desirable socially any more.

Human beings thrive as social beings, part of a context, starting with the bonds that infants form with their parents and other caretakers. Our natural human tendency is to form connections. We have a strong need to affiliate with others.

The social part of life—interaction with our family and friends—diminishes for the elderly. Mrs. Harrington cannot get around as easily as she used to. Neither can her elderly friends. When Tim and Barbara are "flying around all the time," not only does she feel the loss of participation in the family, but she also loses their help in getting out to see her few remaining friends.

Older people aren't as meaningful to others as they once were. They're no longer actively fulfilling their old social and occupational roles. Their sense of *mattering,* of making a difference, is eroding. They want to mean something significant to somebody, but the old, beloved ties and connections are slipping away.

The old are invisible in this society. We look at the wrinkled faces and bent bodies and we forget about the souls inside. We fail to appreciate the accumulated wisdom, the graciousness acquired in an earlier, kinder time.

In dealing with our own feelings of frustration and bewilderment —"Where did I go wrong with Mom"—we have to look for the reasons behind Mom's behavior.

Older People Find Ways to Fight Back

If you felt that society was stereotyping you, treating you in ways that have little to do with who you really are, cutting you off from the mainstream, you'd resent it. You'd find a way around that stereotype. You'd fight back.

This is what our parents are doing. They're finding ways to *compensate* for the losses life has dealt them. The way they go about compensating may be distasteful, embarrassing, and upsetting to us, such as older women painting on bow lips in an effort to recapture their lost youth or older men inflating past accomplishments to gain attention. But the *reasons* for the inappropriate behavior are valid. Our elderly parents and loved ones are trying to make up for what is gone.

All too often, their sexual, occupational, and social diminishments are so overwhelming, so defeating, that our parents retreat into depressed behavior. The older depressed person feels that she is not being cared for. And through her tears and sad demeanor she's trying to gain our sympathy and support.

The melancholic parent may insist she has outstanding children who are "so good to me," but she doesn't really believe it. Where are they now when she needs them? Perhaps in the past she was able to hide her unhappiness, to push it to the back of her mind while she kept busy. But with diminishing capabilities, her emotional floodgates open.

Children with a depressed older parent often find themselves in an emotional hurricane—victims of "water power." They keep trying to please. But as Barbara Harrington puts it, "Nothing we do is enough. She wants more, more! When will it end?"

The answer is never. We can't change another's history or the way she looks at life. A twenty-year-old martyr who keeps stacking up unspoken reproaches will have a large pile of real and imagined hurts and slights by the time she reaches seventy.

Seeing Beneath the Reproaches

The old and weak have tremendous power to make us feel like "dirty dogs." But we can uncover what's really going on, what our parents' hurt looks, crying, and bursts of anger are all about.

Once we learn to see beneath our parents' reproaches, we can distinguish between their very real sexual, occupational, and social losses and the blame they put on us. It's time to do away with our knee-jerk guilt reflexes. We don't *have to* leave a conversation with Mother with palms sweating and temples pounding. We don't *have to* lie awake at night wondering what we did wrong.

The first step in surviving our aging parents is to free ourselves of needless guilt—to understand what is and what is not our fault. We are not to blame for their loss of mate, their diminishing physical powers, or their dwindling circle of friends. The losses of old age are an inevitable fact of life. While we can and should mourn our parents' losses, blaming ourselves for the fact that they are aging only weakens our ability to help and love them.

Mourning Our Parents' Losses

When we see the undeniable signs of aging in our parents' faces and bodies, it hurts. One woman whose father was a highly respected surgeon says, "I remember my father's hands as strong, always careful, methodical. When I was growing up, we kids sensed our Dad was something special. I used to look at those long, strong fingers and imagine they had secret power. Last week he made me a cup of tea, and his hands trembled as he poured. It was painful to watch the change in him."

We hurt because we care. Watching our parents lose their abilities is so upsetting that some of us try to turn away from it. We're so determined to believe that our parents will go on forever that we deny the evidence of their losses. We won't permit them to grow old. This places a terrible burden on the older person who'd like nothing more than to be accepted and respected for who he is, despite the visible signs of aging.

Elisabeth Kübler-Ross, M.D., made a landmark contribution to our knowledge of the mourning process in her book *On Death and Dying*. She has helped us to see what actually happens when we grieve. Working with dying people, Dr. Kübler-Ross was able to isolate five distinct stages of mourning. Kübler-Ross's work is useful in understanding how we react to and mourn our parents' growing old.

Denial and Isolation. "No, no, that's not happening to my mother. Mom is as spry as ever. She's just been feeling a little under the weather lately." We invent all sorts of elaborate reasons to keep reality from entering our consciousness. In this initial stage of mourning, we block what's happening before our eyes. Like little children who cover their eyes so the bad giant won't see them, we take refuge in hiding.

As Kübler-Ross points out, initial denial serves an important function. The patient who learns he is dying needs a buffer between the shock of hearing the news and eventually learning to deal with it. In mourning our parents' failing powers, denial is our buffer until we learn to face reality.

But when we deny, we isolate our parents. We don't allow them to express their feelings about slowing down, about coming to grips with this last part of life. They feel alone and shut out because we're not able to accept what's happening. It's not that we are being cruel or unfeeling. Denial is natural as we begin the mourning process. It's difficult to accept the fact that our once-omnipotent parents, the first and most powerful forces in our lives, are now in need of our support. As we travel farther on the road to acceptance, we learn to face the situation and handle the changed circumstances.

Anger. When our parents' growing frailty can no longer be denied, our feelings of anger, rage, envy, and resentment take over. One middle-aged woman says, "When Mama first moved to a nursing home, I used to have lunch at a little place across the street. A woman my age and her elderly mother often would be there. They'd have shopping parcels with them and be talking and laughing. I'd feel such unreasonable rage that I couldn't eat. 'Why me?' I'd ask myself. 'Why can't I enjoy shopping and having lunch with my mother?' I envied them so much. I'd think of Mama the way she is now, not sure where she is much of the time, and I'd feel cheated. Why was I denied the chance to enjoy my mother's older years? Of course, I'd walk out of the restaurant carrying a thousand pounds of guilt for all my unworthy feelings. I finally solved it. I don't go to the restaurant any more."

Of course we feel angry. Inwardly we seethe. Why isn't our parent growing old gracefully? Why are we made to feel responsible for all her physical and emotional ills? Why us?

In this second stage of mourning, our anger is so all-encompassing that it frightens us. "What's happening to me? I was never this kind of person with these awful feelings. How dare I feel resentment toward my own mother?" Guilt follows anger and we feel worse than ever. We resolve never to feel that way again, but during the very next phone call to Mom, the anger bubbles back up.

It helps to understand that anger is a natural reaction to loss. When you've won most contracts you went after this year, you're not going to feel happy about the one you lose, are you? You're going to feel resentful and envious of the competitor who bagged the contract. You won't show it, but you'll feel it. When we love someone, we're upset when they change. We see our parents getting ready to depart; worse still, their departure leaves us to take over as the older generation.

First, we must admit our anger, understand the sources of it, accept it as an important stage in our mourning. Then we can work through it and not let it damage our relationship with our parents.

Bargaining. When we're going through a traumatic time, many of us bargain with God or some vaguely acknowledged higher power. "I'll be good if you'll let me do what I want." In mourning our parents we strike bargains with God, silently promising to live exemplary lives if God will just take Mother before she becomes senile or suffers a protracted fatal illness. It's childish behavior, of course, based on what we learned to do as children. Our rational side knows that we're indulging in magical thinking, but we still hope and still try to strike bargains.

Depression. In her work with dying patients, Dr. Kübler-Ross characterized the unique sadness of people who are leaving the world. After the denial and pretense, after the enormous rage and despair, after the attempts to work a deal with God, her patients became profoundly sad. Their loved ones reached the same point when all of their other defenses no longer worked.

For us, it is normal to feel sad as our parents grow older. We grieve for two losses: the past, when our parent was a healthy, robust person, and the future, when our parent will grow weaker and finally die. We can't run away from this stage of mourning or shut off our sad feelings. We must recognize our feelings for what they are, allow ourselves to feel "down," and then gather our strength and begin to deal with the last stage of mourning.

Acceptance. When we finally reach this stage, we make peace. Flailing against an unjust situation, trying to bargain our way out of it, allowing our sadness to dominate our lives—none of these tactics will work. Now we are ready to accept the fact of our parents' aging, know that they are not going to grow younger and be as they once were. There is no magic wand that will restore the Mom or Dad of the old days. They are what they are today, and we are the flawed human beings we are. And taking all of our combined faults into consideration, now we can deal with what we have. Now we know that they're not going to change for the better; all our denial, anger, bargaining, and depression won't make any difference. We have mourned for what is gone and cannot be retrieved. As one young single woman answered when she was asked if she were over an angst-filled love affair, "What's next?"

In the next chapters we'll concentrate on practical steps toward positive relationships with our aging parents. When we don't let them "pull our strings," when we can figure out their game plan, when we stop reacting with the classic guilty kid's nervous stomach, then we'll have freed ourselves to love and help our parents.

T W O

Missed Signals

When we're facing our parents across a generation gap, we desperately try to communicate. Some of us report disturbing recurrent dreams in which we're reaching for a parent who's drifting away in a ship or standing on the other side of a deep gorge and calling to us. Our feelings of frustration and helplessness follow us into our sleep.

When we're with our parents, we talk, but we leave with the sense that we didn't really communicate. If we take time to sit back and analyze our pounding heads and churning stomachs, we realize we've just put in two hours of talking at each other—two adults sending words across a void.

Stuart Olsen's eighty-two-year-old father, Dan, lives in a retirement condo in Florida. Always a taciturn man, his one joy was river fishing in the Ohio town where he and his late wife, Georgina, raised the family. He just can't get the hang of fishing for marlin while bobbing around in choppy water. He can't even handle those metal poles with the fancy reels and all. Give him a nice reed pole, a good, flat-bottomed, two-man rowboat, and a calm, slow-running river. Why, when his Stuart was a boy, they'd sit for hours in a rowboat, just enjoying the day.

Stuart and Marj Olsen live in Tulsa. Stu's had several job changes over the years. When you're a sales rep, you can't settle back and wait for your pension, the way his Dad did with the post office. You have to be "on" all the time; there's always a younger guy nipping at your heels, ready to cut into your territory. Every winter, when Stu's business is slow, he and Marj head down to Florida for ten days.

Stu is growing more anxious about Dan, as his father shows signs of frailty. During Stu's annual visits, he tries hard to improve Dad's life.

"How's it going, Dad? Getting any fishing done? I hear they're pulling in some big ones a few miles north of here."

Dan tightens his lips. "Can't fish any more. Too hard on my knees."

"So what about the guys down at the senior center? You used to be a fair poker player. You ever get together with them?"

"Bunch of old men," Dan says. "Some of 'em can't even remember their cards. I'm better off alone."

Desperately, Stuart tries another tack. "Last time you told us a couple of widows in the building were bringing in casseroles, asking you over to watch TV. Anything happening with them?"

Dan glares at his son. "What do I want with them? I had your mother. There's no other woman for me."

Stuart feels his blood pressure rising. But he refuses to give up. "Well, listen, Dad, sounds to me like you're lonely. You need to get out more. How about renting a boat tomorrow and going for a look at that fishing spot up north?"

Dan responds: "What are you talking about? I'm not lonely. And I'm not going in any fancy boat either. You want to fish, go by yourself."

A stand-off. Lately, the Olsens' visits always end this way. As he ages, Dan Olsen sinks further into his silent world. Stuart tells Marj, "I feel as though he's putting up a wall against me. Why can't we talk to each other?"

I'll Talk If You'll Listen

Stuart thinks he's having a conversation with his father, but it's more of a monologue. When Dan rejects his suggestions, Stuart doesn't stop to figure out why. He just jumps to another idea; and they're all Stu's conceptions of what will make his father happy.

Stu's missing the signals behind his father's words. Beneath what Marj refers to as "Dad's litany of complaints" are Dan's true feelings. Communication specialists call these underlying motivations "meta-talk," the meaning behind ordinary words.

Stu listens to the words and reacts to what Dan says. Instead of trying to analyze why his father is so negative, he's busy dreaming up his next argument. Like many salesmen, Stu is positive that the right phrase will sell the customer. We're all guilty of trying to convince, to win a point, while forgetting to *reflect,* to think about what words mean.

In his tight-lipped way, Dan's sending out signals. He won't fish because he gets dizzy spells out on the pier and seasick in the open water. But Dan has never admitted to a weakness in his life. He's not about to start now, and certainly not to his own son. Who's the father here, anyway?

So Stu and Dan face each other across a widening gap. Dan's frightened by his growing weakness and loneliness, and he masks it with crabbiness and exaggerated independence. Stu is too busy thinking of a new way to improve his father's life to reflect on the feelings hidden beneath Dan's curmudgeonly behavior.

Our Buttoned-up Parents

Our older parents grew up with communicating styles typical of their era. "Nice people" did not openly express resentment, anger, lust, and other messy feelings in public.

The meanings of things were obscured, veiled—all wrapped up in an elaborate system of vocal nuance and gesture. To call things the way they are simply was not done. A breast was a bosom. Sexual organs were designated by a rich panoply of euphemisms. And only the lower echelon of society swore in front of women.

Nice people didn't let it all hang out.

Being in control, holding in one's emotions, not washing dirty linen in public—these were all-important values to our parents.

Anne Weinberg recalls when her Aunt Lucille became pregnant with her fourth child. "Everyone in the family acted as though Sadie had made an unfortunate mistake. Four children! In the throes of

World War II, with Uncle Carl wondering if, four kids or not, he'd be drafted into the armed forces. Poor Lucille waddled around, hugely pregnant, and it was never discussed in front of the children. When I asked what the baby would be named, I got the kind of look from my mother that threatened severe punishment if I said another word."

Anne remembers those tense days as a time of raised eyebrows, uncomfortable silences, and dark looks at Uncle Carl, the villain. "Nobody ever talked about it. One day Aunt Lucille was crying onto our kitchen table. My brother and I were sent out of the room with strict orders to disappear. And late that night Lucille went off to the hospital to have the baby. It was so strange. After the baby was born, everyone kind of relaxed, but once I heard my father tell my mother, 'Carl is not a gentleman.'"

For that restrained generation, one's body was a private matter. It was acceptable to talk about one's appearance and even some bodily parts—legs and arms, for instance. But inner workings were not a subject for polite conversation.

Catherine Ori had a hysterectomy for uterine cancer at the age of 84. Her many grandchildren took turns visiting at the hospital.

"How you feeling, Gramma?" Jennifer would ask.
"Oh, as well as can be expected."
"Does it hurt you?"
Catherine would turn her head and look out the window.
"Are you in pain, Gramma? Did you tell the nurse?"

Catherine would shake her head and change the subject. She didn't discuss her "insides" when she was a young woman, and she was not about to do so now.

After several of these visits from her grandchildren, Catherine informed her sons and daughters, "Tell them to stay home. I need my sleep."

The family was getting worried. Gramma Ori, that boundless fountain of grandmotherly love, was shutting them out. She wasn't acting like herself at all.

But Catherine Ori was acting exactly "like herself"—it was not nice to talk about bodily functions, and certainly not malfunctions.

Can We Talk?

Our parents' ideas of "relating" to their kids may differ widely from ours. In our parents' day, communicating with their children was often way down on the priority list after feeding, clothing, educating, and keeping them healthy and out of trouble.

As for understanding us, walking in our shoes, keeping channels of communication open, some parents just were not able to talk straight to us. For them, children were to be seen and not heard.

For the most part, our mothers were free of the thorny problems of the sexual revolution and women's liberation. They perceived their role as helping their daughters become good wives, mothers, and housekeepers and their sons to grow up and make a living.

Many parents never talked to their children about drugs, birth control, abortions, and now AIDS. Things like that happened to other people.

Our generation has been "luckier." Circumstances forced us to open the closed package of parent-child relationships and look at the confronting, angry, tearful, very human mess inside. We have been brought closer to our kids by the times we live in. We have learned to talk about our feelings or lose our children.

It's a Matter of Style

People communicate differently according to personality styles. We send messages about ourselves and our underlying needs by the statements we make. As we age, our personality style often doesn't basically change. The querulous, whining, nine-year-old who's convinced that all the teachers have a grudge against her will most likely believe her boss has it in for her when she enters the business world. And when she's 75, she might be convinced the city's transportation system is rigged against her. Elderly people often become "more of what they were."

Sometimes people adapt to old age by criticizing and bemoaning the modern world. "Things aren't the way they used to be," they tell us. "Nobody cares about doing the job right." It may look as though these older people are simply cantankerous. Actually, they're probably life-long nit-pickers. When the losses and debilities of old age set in, they find fault with the outside world to make themselves feel better. Putting down modern life makes them feel "up."

Criticizing their children is a way of maintaining authority over us. Maybe they can't directly tell us what to do any more because we won't listen. But they can find fault with what we do. Dad's nit-picking ability may be the last arrow left in his quiver, and he'll use it mightily.

When Al and Marion Guest bought a new summer house in Lake Lanier, Georgia, they invited Marion's father out to look at it. He'd been in the construction business in his working days, and they wanted an informed opinion.

Arthur, 76 and still "full of beans," gives opinions gladly. He starts in the garage. "What a bunch of foolishness," he mutters as he stares up into the rafters.

"What's wrong, Dad?" Al asks him.

"It's all wrong, that's what's wrong."

Al feels a $5,000 problem looking him in the face. He can tell. The old man looks grim.

"Uh, you mean bad construction?"

"Bad wood, that's what I mean. Bad wood. They should have sealed that wood. You'll get dry rot sure as shooting."

Al gazes up into the rafters, visualizing dry rot marching down the garage walls to destroy his considerable investment.

Al is still worrying about the dry rot when Arthur announces that the windows were hung wrong, and they can expect lots of swelling in humid weather. The driveway has a chipped spot in the concrete that will surely spell trouble in a few years. The kitchen floor slants, and the drywall looks inferior to him. "Trouble," he intones as he works his way through Al's hard-won, brand-new house.

Marion isn't immune from Arthur's searching eye. "Bad layout in this kitchen. You'll never be able to keep it clean—too much traffic through here. You'll be wiping up mud all summer."

Arthur sees himself as the patriarch of the family. All his life people have sought his advice. He sees no reason to quit giving it now. He has a great need to be important, in charge. His gloom-and-doom talk about dry rot and slanting floors is simply his way of telling his kids: "I'm still an important person, and make sure you don't forget it."

Marion says she "can read Dad like a book." She suggests that Al give Dad some specific projects to do, such as calling in one of the workmen from the "old days" to seal and finish the wood in the garage. "It'll involve him, make him feel wanted. You'll see," she tells Al. "Once he takes charge of that project he'll begin to notice all the good things about the house."

A wise daughter responds to her father's needs, not his hurtful criticisms. By giving Arthur a project to do, Marion lets her dad know he's still an important person. She meets his social need to play an active role in the family and his occupational need to contribute the skills he's developed over a lifetime.

Learning to Play a New Ball Game

As our parents grow older and begin to lose the physical and mental capabilities we all took for granted, our relationship enters a new stage. There's a difference between this "rite of passage" and the others in life's journey. This one does not lead naturally to another stage. There is no happy ending.

How do we survive this new relationship? How do we learn to hear what our parents are really saying?

It becomes a lot easier and less threatening when we accept the fact that the picture has changed. If we continue to relate to our folks as though we were all in a time warp, and we were teenagers in need of strong parental hands, we can't possibly achieve true communication.

We're in a new place in their lives and in ours. The more flexible among us will make the transition. The rest of us will have trouble until we figure out what's going on in this new ball game with different rules.

The Hidden Agenda

Janice McConnell, 52, is thoroughly enjoying her empty nest. She and Bill are both hard-working Seattle realtors. They have finally realized a life-long dream of having their own boat on Lake Washington.

Several times lately Bill's widowed mother, Elizabeth, has called just as the couple was sitting down to eat. The sad note in her voice has made them both so uneasy that they have interrupted their meal to drive over to see her.

When they ring the bell, Elizabeth answers the door in full regalia—high heels, earrings, makeup. She greets them with a big smile and insists they have coffee and home-made pastries.

"Funny, she didn't look sick. Or lonely, either, for that matter," Bill says to Janice on the way home through the damp Seattle streets. "She was out all day with the bridge group. I don't get it."

Janice, who remembers some tense early days with her mother-in-law, starts searching for the hidden agenda. First, she rules out an actual physical problem: Elizabeth's doctor confirms that Mrs. McConnell is in excellent condition. Next, she makes a few discreet inquiries among the family. "Is Mom acting okay? Do you think she's depressed?"

Mom's behavior is mystifying, and it's getting worse. Elizabeth begins calling almost every night. Then, one Sunday when the boat's being repaired, the couple invite Mom over for a leisurely brunch. She arrives looking cheerful as ever and announces, "Well, I bet you're glad you don't have to drag up to the lake this weekend. You can stay here in your beautiful house and relax."

Janice catches Elizabeth's hidden agenda immediately: "You're not paying enough attention to me since you bought yourselves that fancy new boat."

This is so untypical of the independent Elizabeth McConnell that Bill refuses to believe it at first. But Bill still sees the indomitable Mom of his youth, not the aging, sometimes fearful woman Elizabeth is now.

If we allow ourselves to see the *reality* of an older parent's changed situation, we find the clues to the hidden agenda.

Maybe Mother's motive is as simple as getting back at you for something you did thirty years ago. Or, more likely, she's reacting to personality traits she didn't like then and really can't stand now. Our parents love us, but they don't always like us. And they certainly don't like everything we do.

Mrs. McConnell always resented Bill's aggressive, free-wheeling style. "Billy gets what he wants out of life," she used to say with a mixture of pride and a little envy. The fact was, Billy was the one child she couldn't mold. He was a good son, a respectful child, but he never did what she told him to do—even married Janice instead of that lovely Daley girl down the block.

There's no way we can erase those long-standing grudges or magically do away with Mom's need to "stick it to us." But we can be aware of our parents' feelings and learn to protect ourselves. If we suspect we're the object of the "needle," then we must develop tough skins and not let the needle penetrate too far. Presenting a deaf ear can be enormously helpful when your parent is still angry at you for the way you threw your oatmeal across the kitchen.

Who Needs Money?

Our parents often feel the shortage of funds. People living on fixed incomes, drawing from a pension that seemed generous ten or fifteen years ago, have to cut corners.

And because they're part of the "buttoned-up generation," they have great difficulty in talking about money and their fears of what will happen to them when it's gone. Their parents went through the Great Depression. They remember hearing about bread lines and soup kitchens, where former businessmen wore velvet-collared topcoats while standing in line for food to keep them alive. They heard their own parents talk about respectable families whose furniture and belongings were piled up on the sidewalk in front of their homes and families doubling and tripling up in apartments. Some of them went on public assistance to keep their families fed and clothed. Others worked three and four jobs to keep from taking a handout.

It's a matter of pride. People of our parents' generation don't want to be a burden to us, and this feeling extends to the world at large. Many older people refuse to use senior citizen housing or social facilities because, to them, these are handouts. And a handout means that you've failed to provide for yourself. Our parents, despite their varying ethnic backgrounds, are products of the classic American dream: make it on your own and don't take any "free lunches."

"I'd rather die than go to my son," Mr. Kreschefski tells his pal, Mr. Morton, whom he regularly meets on a park bench in a decaying section of Brooklyn.

Mr. Morton eyes his friend's shabby coat and rundown shoes, replicas of his own fading wardrobe. "So if you don't get a new pair of shoes with no holes in the soles, you'll get pneumonia and you *will* die."

"I've got a wonderful son. He works hard for his family. I wouldn't take the bread out of their mouths."

But Mr. Kreschefski's son Barry gets a different message: "Dad, where's the new sweater I brought you? This one's full of holes."

"I like this one. This is good enough. When you're old, you don't need new clothes. I have everything I need."

What looks and sounds like peculiar behavior on the part of the elderly is often an attempt to conserve money. In fact, Mr. Kreschefski is saving the new sweater to wear this winter in the house, when he will keep the thermostat down—fuel costs money.

If we suspect our parents need money but are waiting for them to tell us, we're avoiding the inevitable. Don't listen to "everything's fine." Be alert for the other, nonverbal signs of diminished resources—when Mother fires the cleaning lady and insists—"I do a better job." Or you notice that Dad's once immaculate wardrobe is looking tatty. Or your parents have stopped going to movies or out to eat.

For many older people, growing old in America means teetering on the edge of poverty. The signs are there if we're willing to look.

Stop Nagging—I Took My Medicine

Older people who've been "strong as a horse" in their earlier years often resent the regimen of taking pills each day. The medicine bottles lined up on the kitchen counter may represent a sign of aging, of losing control over one's life. Seniors may convince themselves they don't need the medication and conveniently "forget" to take it.

Pam Lyman's mother never discusses her feelings about taking blood pressure medicine, but her astute daughter notices signs of puffing around her mother's ankles.

"Are you taking your pills, Mom?"

Sweet-faced Dorothy gives her best Norman Rockwell old-lady imitation: "Of course, dear. I always take my medicine first thing in the morning. Dr. Kavnar says I'm the picture of health."

Pam goes into the bathroom, shuts the door, and checks the medicine cabinet. There she finds a full bottle of pills, the very bottle Pam bought more than a month ago.

She faces her mother, "the picture of health." "Well, it seems to me you've had a little oversight here. I see a full bottle of pills in the bathroom. I can't stop here every day on my way to work, so I guess I'll have to ask your neighbor to come in to give you the medicine."

Dorothy is outraged. "I'm perfectly capable of taking my own medicine!"

"Okay," her daughter agrees. "You certainly should be in charge of your own life. What would you think if I bought you one of those new pill counters with a beeper? It would remind you each morning to take your pills."

"Well, I could probably use something like that," her mother agrees.

Pam came up with a reasonable solution. She can monitor her mother's medication by checking the pill counter periodically. And her mother will still maintain a measure of control. Virginia is a "wise child who knows her own parent." She listened not to the story Dorothy fabricated but to the meaning between the lines. And she solved the medication problem in a spirit of cooperation, avoiding a tug-of-war over who should be the boss.

When communicating—or failing to communicate—with our parents, it helps to remember what it's like to deal with adolescents. Individuals at both ends of the generational scale manufacture remarkably similar smokescreens to ward us off. We have to be alert to their tactics and counter them—with strategies that respect our parents' struggles to maintain their dignity and independence in the face of growing frailty.

Don't Worry About Me

Our parents often tell us "not to worry" when they're afraid, feeling unloved, or trying to cope with a whole raft of other intertwined feelings. In classic parental double-talk, "don't worry about me" means "you better worry about me, just in case you're not."

Betty Matsumoto's parents are in their late eighties and still living on their own. By the time mother Moriko reached 80, she had refined a life-long pattern of self-effacement into such a fine art that Betty is fighting incipient ulcers.

Every evening after leaving her job as a graphic designer, Betty dutifully calls the folks. And twice a week she and her husband visit, bringing groceries and cooked foods, handling laundry, and answering the mail.

Ashiro, Betty's father, has been an irascible, disagreeable man for as long as Betty can remember. In old age he contents himself with complaining about everything. Betty manages to tune him out.

But her mother is another story.

"How are you, Mother?" Betty inquires.

Every time she sees her mother she resolves not to ask, and every time she breaks the promise to herself.

In her soft, breathless voice, Moriko says, "My feet don't move. I can't walk at all. Yesterday I almost fall down." Moriko stands to illustrate her weakness and totters backward. Betty and Jim lunge to catch her in time.

Triumphantly, Moriko sinks into a chair. "See?"

"Mother, you must tell Dr. Wayne. Did you call him?"

"Oh no, I don't bother him. He's a busy man."

Jim says firmly, "If you don't call him, we will."

Moriko nods. "Okay. You call. And please tell him I don't breathe at night."

Don't breathe at night! This is a new one. Betty's stomach begins to churn.

Jim steps in again. "Mother, if you didn't breathe at night, you wouldn't be alive. Of course you breathe."

"Maybe you right. I only stop breathe sometimes. Then it start again and I okay."

As they are leaving for home that evening, Moriko stands at the window of the little flat and waves forlornly. "Don't worry about me," she calls. "I fine."

Moriko is living with an ailing, difficult husband and trying to cope with her own increasing physical problems. At this stage in her life, she needs compliments, words of encouragement that assure her she's done a wonderful job all these years. And she desperately needs attention just for herself. She wants her share of the attention pie and is unconsciously orchestrating the script so her kids will worry.

What can Betty and Jim do? They can listen to Moriko's pleas, hidden, as they always have been, behind a mask of self-effacement. Jim can bring a single iris, Moriko's favorite flower, or a book on flower arranging—things that are specifically for Moriko and not for Dad. Or Betty can arrange to take her mother out to a Saturday lunch or an early weekday dinner, making it clear that the outing is "just for the girls." And they can both guide their conversations so that they positively reinforce Mom – talking about Moriko's accomplishments, highlighting her steadfast dedication to home and family, letting her know that she is appreciated. Moriko is questioning whether all her sacrifices have been worthwhile. She needs to know that they have been.

Where Does It Hurt?

Sometimes it hurts too much to hear what senior people are telling us. It hurts to admit that our loved ones are failing. We feel cheated, betrayed—how dare they do this to us? And sometimes we're embarrassed by what we consider inappropriate behavior.

Bernice Saunders is 70. When her mother died, she was only 12, so she has relied upon her older sister Edith, now 80, her whole life. But Edith is suffering memory loss and has many physical ailments, including a poorly functioning bladder.

Edith lives in a retirement home in Sun City, Arizona, with other elderly ladies. They all have severely diminished abilities, and they're all fashion-conscious, dressing up for dinner in the community dining room, wearing jewelry and makeup. Looking nice is an important concern on Edith's floor.

Bernice dislikes the way Edith's white "hospital stockings" look with her orthopedic shoes. So she has bulldozed Edith into wearing slacks, even though slacks are hard for Edith to handle while she attends to her toileting, and they tend to interfere with the walker she must use.

"Those white stockings are awful!" Bernice tells Edith. "They make you look like an old lady. Wear the slacks I bought you."

"But I am an old lady," Edith reminds her. "I just can't manage slacks any more."

And so the argument goes at every visit.

Bernice has great difficulty accepting Edith's changed circumstances. When the sisters were growing up, Edith, as older sister, was the family caretaker, advice-giver, tower of strength. Bernice was the pretty, fluttery one. When she had a problem with a boyfriend or a fight with their father, she'd go to Edith for "straightening out."

Tiptoeing into the "golden years" herself on her expensive Italian shoes, Bernice is not ready to accept Edith's "old-ladiness." And Bernice's inability to move to this new stage is giving both of them a hard time. Edith is trying to tell Bernice the truth: "Look, I have diminished abilities and I have to adjust to them." But Bernice can't hear it.

When we're dealing with the frustrations and conflicting emotions that the aging of our parents and loved ones brings into our own lives, we forget that we have some control over the situation. True, we can't bring back their youth or health. But we can learn to deal with who they are now. We can look behind behavior we don't like and words that turn us off. We can find that kernel of personhood that's hiding behind the facade. And we can start by listening and responding to what our parent is trying to tell us: "I'm still here. I need your love and attention. I need to know I count. I need to know I can make it to tomorrow."

THREE

Sending Straight Signals

In the last chapter we talked about reading your parent's actual agenda—getting a handle on the "meta-talk" behind the words, knowing what a shrug or downcast eyes or a flood of tears really means.

Now that we're "experts" in reading the signals, how do we send straight signals back? Good communication with our parents begins by following a few basic rules.

Rules of the Communicating Game

Pick a time and place when you won't be distracted. If you're standing in the kitchen looking through bills and Mom is calling out complaints from the living room, your communication technique will leave a lot to be desired.

Let Mom vent. Chances are she's alone a great deal. She needs an audience besides the philodendron and the cat.

Be truly attentive. Even if your parent provides you with an "organ recital" of all the latest ills, the list of complaints will be exhausted eventually. Your parent may feel reassured just by telling you about a new pain or ache. People of any age who live alone tend to be more upset about physical ailments. When one awakens at 2 A.M. with a pounding heart and sweaty palms, it seems worse when the other side of the bed is empty.

Show you're listening. Look Mom or Dad in the eye, nod your head encouragingly, insert a few judicious "ummm, hmmns," smile. Let your face react to your parent's words.

Repeat what your parent just said. Your repetition assures that you're registering what your parent is telling you.

Don't pass judgment even if you're right. If you think Dad's feelings about the janitor or a "nasty young clerk"are exaggerated, maybe even bordering on paranoid, bite your tongue. They're his feelings. Right or wrong, he's entitled to have them.

Remember that you're having a conversation between two equals. Don't dismiss or "pooh-pooh" Mom's comments. She may be in worse shape physically than you are; she may be out of touch with the times we live in; but she's telling you her side of things. And that's just as valid as yours.

Don't condescend and don't patronize. Although Mother may seem a bit childish at times (don't we all?), you're not talking to a child. Many staff members in hospitals and nursing homes speak v-e-r-y clearly and loudly to senior people. Cognizant of the frequent hearing and comprehension losses among the elderly, they treat all oldsters as less-than-bright six-year-olds. There is nothing more demeaning than to be spoken to in this way. If you have to raise your voice to get Dad to hear you, do it. But don't also assume he can't understand you.

Free Advice Has a Price Tag

If your parent doesn't ask you for advice, don't give it. "Free" advice carries its own price tag. You resent it when your parents try to tell you how to run your life. To our parents, we seem more than a little presumptuous when we offer words of wisdom they haven't asked for.

Alicia, 45 and unmarried, came home from a business trip to Belgium one day, threw down her Burberry raincoat, and collapsed on the couch.

Her hopes for a quiet evening exploded when her widowed mother, Grace, a vivacious 67, called to say that she'd met "someone fabulous" while Alicia was away.

"We're getting married!" Grace announced breathlessly.

"Not so fast!" Alicia burst out. "Who is this man? You hardly know him."

Suddenly Alicia became a sage advice giver. She conveniently forgot her days of following a rock musician around the country, once calling home for bail money for her unstable boyfriend.

Her mother was making a drastic mistake—it was Alicia's duty to stop her!

Alicia failed to appreciate the feelings underlying Grace's words. Grace had been alone for nine years. She was lonely. She'd met a man she wanted to marry. And she wanted her daughter to be happy for her.

Alicia approached the impending marriage with the same attitude she brought to her corporate job. This situation called for management by objective. With proper management, Alicia believed she could stop the marriage.

Despite Alicia's best efforts, Grace and Harold, a retired Social Security clerk, got married. Since both bride and groom lived on moderate fixed incomes, they pooled their resources and talked openly about how they managed their budget.

Alicia was relieved that Harold had not married her pretty mother for her money. Still, she was uneasy about the way the couple lived. They moved to a less desirable part of town to save money and shopped at discount supermarkets on Senior Discount Days.

"I found a much nicer apartment in the Bay Ridge area," Alicia told Grace one day. "It's only $25 more a month than the one you have, and it has central air conditioning. I told the super to hold it until you looked at it."

Her easy-going mother turned on Alicia, face red and eyes brimming with tears. "I'm sure you mean well, dear, but for heaven's sake, let me make my own decisions!"

"Let me make my own decisions"—how often Alicia had hurled those words at her parents when she was exploring the byways of "finding herself."

Fortunately, Alicia had a long memory. She remembered her resentment at all the unsolicited advice her parents had given her when she was young. And she was sensitive enough to her mother's feelings to see that she had tapped an emotional wellspring. Graciously, Alicia altered her "management" style to one of benign neglect.

Oh, You Poor Baby

We're touched by the plight of a failing parent. We watch as Mother's hands shake when she pours us tea, or we see the network of wrinkles on Dad's face—and we get a lump in our throats. We care about these people, and we want them to know that.

The trick is to show our caring, concern, and compassion without expressing pity.

Children who are overprotected have difficulty developing self-reliance. They begin to think, "Hmmmm, maybe I'm really a helpless baby. Maybe I can't cope."

By the same token, we don't want to smother our mother with "Poor Baby" platitudes. When we do, we're suggesting she really is a hopeless old wreck and has good reason to feel bad about herself.

In psychological terms, we want to show we care, but we don't want to *reinforce* feelings of worthlessness and the bad behavior that results from them.

Julia Marek got a late-night long distance call from her brother in St. Louis. Her mother, Clara, had fallen and broken her hip.

By the time Julia made flight connections from the small northern California town where she and her artist husband lived, the surgery had been done.

Julia arrived at the hospital in time to see her mother sitting up in bed with a pink ribbon in her hair. Clara had been a "tough cookie" all her life—raising two kids on a widow's pension plus any decent work she could find. Usually clad in jeans and sneakers, Clara was not much for pink ribbons. She was 78 and still grew her own vegetables. In fact, she'd fallen on a spade while she was planting radishes.

Julia and her brother Sam attributed Clara's apparent weakness and lassitude to the surgery. But when a week went by and Clara still spoke in a wispy voice and still had that pink ribbon in her hair, Julia got a little worried.

"We simply love your mother," the nurses crooned. "She's the best patient we have. What a love she is. So sweet and easygoing."

Julia and Sam wouldn't have characterized their tough little mother that way.

The days went by and Clara continued to lie in bed, smiling at the nurses. Once she caught a young, lively nurse by the hand and said to Julia, "This one is my very favorite. She braids my hair."

"They're making a baby out of her! And she loves it!" Julia confided to Sam. "What'll we do?"

Sam shrugged. "I don't know. She'll get over it, once she's walking and back in her own house."

But Julia was too worried to let it go at that. She had to get back to her job and family soon. She felt she had to snap her mother out of it before she left. Sam would just ignore the whole thing.

"Ma, I think you're letting the nurses pamper you too much. It's not good for you. You're used to being independent."

"I'm a sick woman! They understand me better than you do. They know how to treat me. At least they show how they like me!" Clara gestured toward the bow in her hair.

"But Ma, you're not a baby. I love you too. You know that. I just want you to get well." Julia pleaded.

Clara shook her head. "I'm too sick. You don't understand. They know I'm sick. That's why they're so nice to me." Eventually, even the sweetest nurses had to toughen up on Clara, force her out of bed and make her walk. There came a day when the nurses were too busy to brush her hair. That day, Julia noticed, there was no pink ribbon in Clara's hair. She told Julia, "I can't wait to get out of this place."

Say It Right

When we send out our own signals, it's important that we say what we want to say in ways that make our parents feel better. In psychological terms, our words should be *ego-syntonic*. In layman's terms, we might call our language "stroking for a good reason."

Ideally, the ego-syntonic statement will leave an afterglow. After you've left, your parent should feel, "I'm glad I spoke to my daughter. I feel better now." A good ego-syntonic statement hits us where we live. It taps into the listener's deepest fears and anxieties and allays them.

Suppose your father is grumbling about how slow he is, how he can't do what he used to do. You can give him food for thought by telling him, "I'm proud of what you've done with your life. You can look back on all your accomplishments with a good feeling. And it doesn't matter how slow you are. You do as you always did—the very best you can."

Ego-syntonic words are encouraging words. They're not quick little fixes that deny there's a problem: "You're fine, you're fine. Forget about it."

Sending straight signals doesn't mean "letting it all hang out." If we've always used delicacy and tact when talking with our parents, if we preserved a certain civility, then this is no time to hit them with brutal talk.

Communicating with our parents should be like any other exchange. We've had to learn how to talk to a boss, to a young child, to strangers at a cocktail party. Nobody gets to mid-life without employing the built-in editor in her mind, carefully deleting words or phrases that can wound or be misunderstood.

We have to give some thought to making those statements that leave a lasting impression, that give our aging parents hope. When our uncoordinated eight-year-old was a failure on his class gym team, we encouraged him and praised him for his efforts in the Stamp Club. We looked for other ways to help him cope with the bad time he was having.

This strong need for encouragement, for positive, loving words that sustain and buoy us as we flounder in rough waters, doesn't leave as we age. The need becomes stronger when everything around us is changing and we feel ourselves diminishing. Some seniors not only shrink in actual physical size ("I used to be tall," they tell us), they also feel shrunken, diminished, less than what they were.

I'm Entitled to Feel Miserable!

Louise Whitescarver was the unhappiest woman she knew. Her husband of 57 years just died, she was trying to keep a large apartment going on the small pension that Elton had left her, and her children didn't understand her.

Although she tried, whenever the "kids" visited, their conversations ended with her crying. Louise would sob and sob; her children just stared at her with stricken faces.

Bill, the youngest, was 55 and a successful advertising man. He was generally characterized as "good with people." He knew a lot of jokes and was a fluent conversationalist. But his mother's tears and dejection defeated him. "Come on, Mom, lighten up. Let's go out to lunch. It'll make you feel better."

"I'm not hungry. I can't eat."

But Bill persisted. He and his wife, Marcey, took Louise to one of the most upbeat restaurants they could find. The place was full of plants, young enthusiastic people, and pleasant background music.

Bill told jokes and little stories about his co-workers, and Louise cried.

Marcey tried to cheer her mother-in-law. She was genuinely fond of Louise and remembered when Mom was a light-hearted, charming woman, happy with Elton and interested in her children's lives. "Mom, there's a fashion show at Neiman-Marcus Monday. Let's go. Debbie will be home from college, and we can have a girls' day out. How about it? It'll make you feel better."

Louise shook her head. "No. I'm not ready for that yet."

Bill chimed in. "Come on, Mom, a day with Marcey and Deb will do you a world of good."

But Louise knew her own feelings. She was sad and depressed. She missed Elton terribly and just wasn't ready.

Bill and Marcey meant well. But they were so uncomfortable about their own feelings that they couldn't recognize or accept Louise's. Their mistake is one we often make when we're faced with a sad, hopeless loved one. We never *talk about their feelings.*

Respecting Feelings

Bill and Marcey's attempts to take Louise's mind off her troubles were really attempts to take their own minds off Louise's troubles. Our tendency is to try to talk our depressed parents out of their feelings. Or we go in the other direction and baby an unhappy elderly person with excessive pampering. Both kinds of behavior may make us feel better, alleviate some of our guilt and anxiety. But they don't address the real problem of how *Mom* is feeling.

We can help if we start by *recognizing* how she's feeling. We make note of her remarks and behavior. We acknowledge her messages and signals.

Next, we *accept* how she's feeling. This is harder than it sounds. Most of our communication problems with our parents stem from our inability to *accept the reality of their feelings.* It would be much easier and more pleasant all around if Mom drifted into old age with a sweet smile on her face. If only she'd act like a greeting-card elderly lady and sit in her rocker, beaming lovingly at her family.

But Mom is not beaming. She's complaining. She's fretful. She's crying. She's negative. She's giving us dirty looks.

In a word, she's unhappy. And when we accept the validity of that feeling, we're on the way to breaking down the barriers between us.

It's vital that we *accept without reinforcing* our parent's negative feelings. If we say, "I guess you feel pretty bad today," we're telling Mom we know how she feels and also that we respect her *right* to feel that way. We're saying, "You've had a bad time. You're entitled to feel sad." But if we carry that a step further and flood her with too much sympathy, we're feeding right into her negative feelings about herself, reinforcing what she's suspected all along. "I knew it!" her unconscious says. "I'm worthless. And they agree with me. Look how they're babying me."

When we accept, we're giving Mom our understanding. And that's what she really wanted all along. When we accept her sadness and despair, we're showing Mom that we're not fighting her, we're not negating her feelings. On the contrary, we're giving her the loyalty she needs. Our message is, "I'm on your side."

Can We Talk?

Once we've given up our vision of the perfect greeting-card elderly lady we fervently hoped our mother would be and have accepted the way she really feels, it frees both of us. We no longer feel compelled to "talk her out" of her feelings, to divert and deflect her. And she, in turn, can drop some of the "front."

Now we're both free to talk. When Mama's tears begin to flow or she stares out the window, we know what to do. We don't ignore her or try to change the subject. We face the fact that she's unhappy. And we give her permission to tell us why if she wishes. If we ask her, "What are you thinking about that's making you so unhappy?" we're telling her that we're willing to talk about it. If she wants to unload, we're here to listen and to hear her out.

Throughout our lives, most of us function with a support system. The people at the golf club, our buddies at work, our childhood friends who know all our faults—they're there when we need to let off steam. But for many older people, that support network is gone. Their friends are ailing or dead. Often, they're widowed or widowered. Their busy doctor really doesn't have time to hear their lists of complaints. They need non-judgmental acceptance of their deepest feelings. And we can give them that.

Sometimes the older person really doesn't want to talk or isn't ready to face his feelings. There's no way we can force him to "tell all." In fact, it would be embarrassing for all of us if we persisted in encouraging Dad to talk when he secretly wants us to stop being so supportive and go home. But we can offer our parent the option— provide the opening by communicating our understanding and our willingness to talk.

Little Things Mean a Lot

We talk about spending "quality" time with our children, our mates, and our friends. We carefully plan special events—such as dinner at a new restaurant—so our time together is stimulating and memorable.

With a little thought, we can expand our parents' worlds and make our times together enjoyable and special.

Push back the walls. If our parents feel "shrunken," some of that feeling is due to the harsh fact that they are living in a shrunken world. Old friends are ill or dead, one's mate may be incapacitated so that outings are few and far between, and it costs money to go places. For the lively senior who has enjoyed moving about and doing new things, enforced relegation to the rocking chair can be overwhelmingly depressing.

When one is confined to a small apartment, even a trip to the supermarket is stimulating and fun; or a stop in a new little coffeeshop; or a good long trip through a home improvement center or hardware store so Dad can check out new gadgets. We need only think of what our parent enjoys to come up with ideas for agreeable outings.

Make contact. People never lose their need for warm, reassuring physical contact. A touch on the hand, a kiss on the cheek, a hug— they all reinforce a feeling of being worthwhile.

For many older women, physical contact answers the nagging question, "Am I still pretty?" It's especially difficult for "head-turners" when they age. They agonize over every spider vein in their once-knockout legs and every age spot on their famous peaches-and-cream complexion. The physical signs of aging knock all of us into momentary depression. If someone we care about gives us a big hug, we feel reassured: "So maybe I'm a wreck; somebody still cares about me."

"Tell me about the good old days." For many older people, the past is very much alive, clear in all its details, and often preferable to the present. Maybe it's boring to hear about our own escapades at the age of ten or how our mother's father used to hold exercise sessions every morning for all the children. But the connection with the past and "what I used to be" is often a vital part of the senior's sense of self.

Occasionally, Mom or Dad really doesn't want to talk about the past. He or she may be one of those people for whom the present is much more fascinating. He'd rather talk about politics or the latest book. If you steer the conversation back to the past too much, he'll let you know: "The past is over. I already did that. Don't try to turn me into one of those old people who can only talk about what used to be."

"What do you *think, Mom?"* Asking your parent's advice is the deepest compliment. It's also an excellent way to keep her from giving unwanted advice! If your mother is too quick to point out your teen-age daughter's shortcomings, overlook that and instead ask Mom to tell you how to make slipcovers or bake the real Swedish pancakes.

We encourage the older parent, draw her into our lives, when we ask advice. "How do you keep the spaghetti from sticking?" "How do you drive a nail into drywall?" And that most important one of all: "Why's the baby crying?" For the failing parent who may not be able to cook for herself or handle many of the tasks she once did, being asked for advice can do wonders to reinforce her self-worth.

Karen Mitterman, 54, couldn't talk with her mother. Whenever they were together, Karen says, "We were explosions waiting to happen." Both women were quick-tempered and outspoken. Their meetings were often confrontational. "Ever since Dad died," Karen says, "I could never leave Mother's house without a clenched stomach or a headache."

But one day, when Karen and her 79-year-old mother were talking about Karen's new grandson, her mother broke into a big smile and said, "I know why that baby is so good-natured."

"Why, Mother?"

"Because your daughter is smart enough to give him a pacifier when he's fussy. You'd never do that when your babies cried."

The implied insult to Karen's abilities as a mother was there, just as it often was, but this time Karen didn't take the bait. "Did you give us pacifiers, Mom?"

"No," her mother admitted, "but I did dip a cloth in sugar water and let you suck on that. It quieted you down. I told Lisa about it, and that's why the baby is so easy to handle."

Pictures of sugar-water cavities raced through Karen's mind. All those awful sessions with the dentist when she was growing up....

Wisely, she dropped the subject. And in the coming months she began to see a softening in her mother. Their conversations began to revolve around how much fresh air a baby needs, if Lisa should be covering his head with a bonnet in the hot sun, at what age her mother thought an infant was ready for vegetables.

Karen's mother had a chance not only to focus on her own skills as a baby expert but to pass on her accumulated wisdom—one of the true joys of old age.

Touching base with the human family. By the time we reach the last part of our lives, we've met and touched a lot of people. We've left marks. It's enormously satisfying to our older parents to tell them when some friend or relative has asked about them. If you ran into Mrs. Morgan in the post office this morning and she asked about your father, make sure you tell him. He may wave it away with, "That old busybody," but it's always nice to know that somebody is remembering.

When you visit, bring a little present from time to time. It needn't be anything elaborate. A few apples, a half-pound of nuts, anything that qualifies as "a favorite." The object means very little— it's the thought behind it. You're showing caring when you give a little gift.

Take pictures, lots of pictures. Why else are there "Grandma's Brag Books," those overpriced little photo albums every grandmother carries in her purse? Pictures establish our connections with each other, and they're absolutely essential to every conversation that begins, "Let me tell you about my grandchildren."

"What's the matter, you broke your hand and you can't write?" If you live in another part of the country, writing notes and cards or dashing off an e-mail message is a good way to show your parents that you're thinking of them. If you're too busy and too tired at the end of the day to write a letter, try sending greeting cards or colorful postcards. These are especially appreciated by people who live in nursing homes. And, of course, you can always telephone and chat about the little details of life. The telephone provides a much-needed connection to the world outside some parents' shrinking circles.

Make your visit more than "just a talk." If your father enjoys checkers, make sure you get out the board and set it up. Or if Mom always loved reading but can't see well enough now, read her the daily paper or magazine articles you think she'll enjoy.

All the things we've talked about in this chapter are merely "how tos" for expressing our care and concern. They're tools for reaching across the generation gap. The ideas we've suggested: spending quality time with your elderly parent, offering a listening ear, giving encouragement, respecting their feelings—apply to all your relationships with friends and loved ones. Sending straight signals is the foundation. The building blocks come next.

FOUR

Status: It's All in the Family

In *Anna Karenina,* Tolstoi made an astute observation about family life: "Happy families are all alike; every unhappy family is unhappy in its own way."

Family dynamics are fascinating. They've inspired our most memorable dramas, from *Oedipus Rex* to *A Streetcar Named Desire.*

The fabric of the family contains many interwoven threads. Each family member tries to assure his own *place;* each family member carries out learned patterns of behavior—his *role*; and everyone is interacting with everyone else.

In aging parent-adult child relationships, problems begin when the parent's place, or *status,* is threatened by failing powers.

Like us, our parents are social animals. All human beings need to be respected and appreciated. That's how we achieve status in our social group.

This compelling need to be accepted and sure of one's place in the social group persists throughout our lives. When a four-year-old sees his parents "slow-dancing" to a favorite record, he wants to be part of it, stake out his place. Teen-agers seek status in their peer group by wearing the "right" jeans or hairstyle. As adults, we get status from a variety of sources: our jobs, volunteer work, and—if that's our style—a bright red sports car.

Older people need status, too. More than that, they're accustomed to having it. Over the years, they've built up a sense of importance, of being necessary. They don't like to be put down, overlooked. They want what they feel is owed them—respect for who they are and what they have contributed.

Our folks gain status from holding some form of power. It can be the ability to control the pursestrings and make decisions about money. Or it can be the skill to bake the best chocolate chip cookies in the universe. Or perhaps it's the right to express one's accumulated wisdom, one's unique storehouse of information about the past and the role one played in it.

Actually, our parents don't have to do anything to gain status. Most families tacitly understand the parents' moral authority. Most of us took in the concept of our parents' importance along with our oatmeal. We were taught to listen to them and respect them simply because they *are* our parents. High on the list of the Ten Commandments is "honoring thy father and mother," and, by and large, most of us try to live up to that. That's why we feel so guilty when we don't listen to them.

One important way our aging parents obtain status is from their children. When we're successful people, carrying out our lives as real honest-to-goodness grown-ups, our parents feel they've done something right. All the jokes about "My Son, the Doctor" are based on the very real assumption that our successes give our folks status.

Aging parent-adult child connections follow various patterns, depending on the degree of status Mom and Dad retain in the family as well as what role the adult children fill in the equation. These patterns are:

1. Status-equality: a relationship in which parent and child function as two adults who relate to each other as friends or colleagues with equal status.

2. Status-quo: a lopsided relationship in which parents hold most of the power and adult children are still under parental control.

3. Status-conflict: a tug-of-war between parent and grown children over rights and power. The conflict comes when parents feel their abilities slipping and don't want to give up status.

4. Status-reversal: the pattern that develops when parents grow weak and dependent upon their adult children.

With a Little Bit of Luck

When we enjoy a peer relationship with our parents, in which they maintain their lives independently of us, that's *status-equality,* and the gods are smiling. In this kind of family, both parents and children maintain status. The ingredient that makes it work is respectful cooperation between the two sides. It's a happy situation, and if we're lucky, it will persist throughout our parents' lives.

Status-equality is most likely to continue as long as two conditions exist: our parents enjoy good health, and they are financially secure. Of course, status-equality also depends upon healthy patterns that we and our parents have built up over time. When it was time to release us from being children, time to view us as equal adults, our parents let us go. They were concerned with our happiness as independent human beings, not as reflections of themselves or subordinates whose reason for being was to serve them.

And we, in turn, left our rebelliousness and anger back in high school.

Probably one of the best examples of successful status-equality takes place when a daughter has her own baby. Mother and daughter, who have had their "ups and downs" over hair, clothes, boys, late hours, and loud music, become friends and confidants. The daughter now discovers that her mother, who had such weird ideas about dating and hairstyles, is absolutely brilliant when it comes to knowing why a baby cries. The baby's peculiar whimpers and sighs in the middle of the night suddenly appear normal and natural when mother says, "Oh yes, they all do that in their sleep. Try rubbing his back gently. It usually works."

Status-equality situations also are likely to develop when the father takes his son into the business. Father and son share the work, each contributing his strengths, as would any set of equal partners. The father, if he's not maneuvering for dominance in the relationship, is able to enjoy all the benefits of his son's partnership.

One of the most interesting equal-partnership situations arises when the son or daughter does not follow in the parent's footsteps but forges ahead into new territory. One Dean of Admissions at a college saw the slipping enrollment figures and knew he'd have to try something new.

He assembled his eager young recruiters and said, "We need to mount a public relations campaign to attract new students. I've got the right person, and it won't cost us a penny. She has volunteered to help and will fly in Friday morning for a 10:00 A.M. meeting." When they all met on Friday morning, he introduced a charming, white-haired woman to his young staff. "I'd like you to meet our consultant," he said. "This is Mrs. Adams, a retired P.R. woman and my mother."

Over the years, this man had worked with his mother in a comfortable, networking relationship. He thought of her as a highly competent colleague and called on her expertise from time to time. In turn, she had often asked his advice on marketing campaigns she was handling for educational institutions.

A status-equality relationship can be as structured as a young doctor entering his or her parent's practice or as casual as a mother and daughter shopping together for new draperies. In each case the older and the younger halves of the partnership value the other person's contributions. One pediatrician in the San Francisco Bay area sums up his relationship with his daughter. "Stacy is a nurse practitioner and I'd hoped she'd join me in my office. But she's really determined to work with Third World countries and has lived in Asia and Africa already. Right now, she's working in a clinic in a mountainous region of Mexico. Do I worry about her? Sure, I do. But I respect what she's doing."

His daughter, on one of her brief trips back to the U.S., explained her feelings about her father. "As long as Dad is healthy and able to handle the practice alone, I'll continue with what I'm doing. But if that changes, I'll consider coming back and joining his practice. We make a good team."

Since nothing in life is ever immutable, some of us will see our status-equality relationship change as our parents become weaker and older. There's a special sadness that we, as children of aging parents, feel when vigorous, "in charge" Mom and Dad move into the rough waters of failing health and dwindling financial resources. Our aging parents need enormous courage and good humor to survive these changes. And so do we! We'll discuss the process of transition in more detail in the next chapter.

Status-Quo Relationships:
Big Daddy (or Mommy) Still Runs the Show

If the aging parent still holds the reins and calls the shots, and the grown-up offspring still operate as "children" subordinate to their parent, that's a *status-quo* relationship. The balance of power hasn't changed since the children were, literally, children. Mom or Dad or both of them were always dominant, perhaps benevolent dictators, and the kids knew their place within that framework. "Status-quo" means that things are going along the way they always did. Our folks still hold enough power of one kind or another (often financial power) to maintain a dominant position in the family.

In a status-quo family script, the family hierarchy is clear. If Dad has been the patriarch, the leader of the family (or Mom has been the matriarch) for as long as you can remember, there are few communication problems.

Your parent lays down the law for the lower echelon to follow; his or her power is simply a fact of family life.

As is true in a status-equality relationship, one common denominator is money. Dad and Mom have enough funds to guarantee control over their own lives. If they want to go south for the winter, then they do as they wish. Or if they need nursing care, they can afford to hire a companion or private nurse without consulting the rest of the family. They're still in charge of these decisions, and their children don't *have to* become involved.

Status-quo relationships may or may not work well for both sides. If the parents are benevolent monarchs (or dictators), and the children are comfortable in their subservient role, fine. Dad perceives himself as strong and independent; the children appreciate his vigor and command of life. They may be grateful for his guidance and direction and relieved that he isn't a "burden" on them.

But sometimes Dad is not a benevolent patriarch. Sometimes he uses his money and independence to manipulate and dominate his children.

The Power Brunch

Every Sunday morning the Martin family meets at The Pancake Castle for brunch. The father, Robert, age 87 and still in full charge of his faculties plus a thriving wholesale leather business, has been conducting these weekly meetings since his wife Margaret died 15 years ago.

Among those in attendance are Elliott, the oldest son (61), his wife, Suzanne (58), and their two married children with their respective spouses. Elliott is in the family business.

Next to the patriarch sits Rick, middle son (59), divorced and considered the "family playboy." Occasionally, Rick's daughters and their husbands join the group. Rick is not in the business. His father describes him as "a man with no head for figures. Rick likes boats." A realist, Elliott is on the mark. Rick makes just enough money to support his leisure-time habits.

Farther down the table sits the "baby" daughter, Kathy (age 55), and her family. Kathy went straight from Daddy's house into a marriage in which she is equally pampered. Her husband, Mark, also works for her father and makes sure Kathy gets the things that make her happy.

At each Sunday morning power brunch, the dynamics are played out over the scrambled eggs:

Robert: "Elliott, did you see the sales figures for last month? You better ride that sales force harder. They're slacking off."

Elliott, who is sales manager, flushes red and mumbles, "I know, I know."

Suzanne, Elliott's wife, says, "Dad, El works very, very hard. That man comes home from work exhausted. Most of the time he's too tired to eat supper."

Robert: "So it won't hurt him to skip a meal. I've missed plenty of dinners. It didn't hurt me." He pats his own skinny stomach. "People eat too much anyway." He glares at Rick, the boater, who is busy spreading butter on his apple pancake.

Rick beams at his family. "Great pancake! When I lived in California, I used to have dreams about this place." Rick has lived in many parts of the country in his quest for the good life.

Robert grunts. The grunt is a successful communication tool for the old man. It's usually critical, and it usually conveys, "See, what did I tell you? You're an idiot."

Kathy reaches a hand across the table and pats Suzanne's arm. "What's wrong? You look sick."

Suzanne rubs her forehead. "I don't know. I must have had too much coffee. I'm getting a headache."

Robert turns to Elliott. "Why don't you take that wife of yours to a doctor? She gets too many headaches."

Kathy's husband Mark whispers to Karen, "Here we go again."

The brunch continues. Elliott squirms on his hot seat as Dad tells him off for transgressions during the past week. Suzanne holds her head. Rick tunes them all out and eats a big meal so he won't have to cook later. Kathy, who always looks nice, makes sure everyone admires the new outfit that Mark just bought her, and Robert congratulates himself on holding together his family.

Money and power go together. In Robert Martin's case, they are the underpinnings of the status-quo family relationship. Besides Robert's financial security and the power of his self-made empire, there is an important third ingredient: he's *independent* of his children.

Robert, the caretaker, does not really believe his "kids" are capable adults. Although he prides himself on his hard-headed realism, he has somehow missed the fact that his children have grown up. Privately, Suzanne refers to her father-in-law as "living-proof that Father Knows Best."

At the age of 61, Robert's son Elliott still feels like a figurehead in the business, without any real authority. No wonder his wife goes home with a migraine after every Sunday brunch.

The scenario of this power brunch follows a similar script at each meeting. But if this family were not locked into a status-quo pattern based on the father's money and power, other patterns could develop. They all have options to play out different roles.

Take Elliott, the one who suffers most from his father's domination. If he had decided to confront his father long ago with a show of power of his own, perhaps he and Robert would now enjoy a relationship approaching status-equality. Elliott chose to prove himself to his dad with long, dedicated hours of work. He was capable and knew it. He felt it was only a matter of time before Robert would recognize his contributions and share leadership. But that day never came. Elliott misjudged Robert; his father never gave up anything without a struggle.

After a few years of seasoning in the business, Elliott could have "creatively" confronted Robert: "Dad, here's my plan for how we can work together and how I can use my marketing skills to increase business." The older son might have discovered that Robert was anticipating just such a confrontation. At that point, they could have begun working on a gradual sharing of power. Of course, given Robert's style and personality, Elliott would have had a major fight on his hands. Did he have the stomach for it? He would have had to possess enough patience to win the old man over eventually.

Elliott had another option. When he saw that his waiting game wasn't working with his father, he could have taken the skills he'd developed and gone to another company. Or he could have started a business of his own. Granted, neither of those courses would have been acceptable to Robert. Elliott might not have been invited to The Pancake Castle for brunch. On the other hand, feisty Robert might have come to respect his older son for being his own man.

The Transfer of Dominion

Many of the conflicts between parents and their adult children center on the *transfer of dominion*, or power, from parent to child. In transferring dominion, the parent is handing over his "lordship," his kingdom, his role. He can still maintain status, but his role has changed.

We transfer power when we hand over the ability to influence. The father who takes his son into the business to allow him to contribute and help him grow in influence is handing over power in a healthy way, appropriate to both the father's and the son's changed positions in life.

Unfortunately, not all parents are prepared to turn over a measure of dominion. Robert Martin is an example of an aging parent who's unwilling to effect a transfer of power to his son. And his son and daughter-in-law (remember her migraine headaches?) are caught in the situation.

There's No Business Like a Family Business

There are good reasons why conflicts over status erupt when a son or daughter is brought into the family business. Dad has been running the business the same way for thirty or forty years. He's developed a whole set of business practices and rules for handling people. Along comes the son with his M.B.A., and sparks fly.

The conflict develops because Dad is not ready to turn over *dominion*.

Often, the father gives lip service. He talks about making life easier for himself, sharing the load with his son (or daughter). But he functions as an overseer, a supervisor of his child's activities, never really allowing the child to be a partner. The father is holding tight to the reins, and his son, with a head full of plans and new ideas, is pulling at the other end.

From the father's standpoint, the conflict is based on his belief that the son just isn't "ready." He needs seasoning in the business and the opportunity to absorb all that the father has learned through experience. He feels the son wants to change things just for the sake of change.

From the adult child's standpoint, Dad's methods are outmoded. He feels he can make a real contribution to the business, perhaps by instituting modern technology. Also, he thinks it's time to make "the old man's life easier." He's ready and willing to put in the ten- or twelve-hour day so Dad can take a long trip with Mom.

Both of them are operating from the purest motives and yet they're tangled in a conflict over status. Sometimes the struggle goes on for years, with a sixty-year-old son or son-in-law still trying to wrest authority from Dad, who hangs on with feeble hands but a will of iron. In some families dominion never does get transferred, even after "Sonny" is ready for retirement.

When we talked about Elliott Martin's problems with his domineering father, we conjectured that in the past Elliott might have been able to get his father to treat him as an equal. But Elliott's game plan was to wear his father down by proving himself. It didn't work for him, but in some families dominion does get transferred. The father eventually "sees the light" and hands over some of the power. This often happens when the all-powerful father begins to have physical problems. He finds himself in a hospital bed with wires and tubes vying for space in his body and he realizes that he won't live forever. It's to his benefit and that of the entire family to start turning over more responsibility to his son. Then the family relationship inches its way from status-quo to one of status-equality. Hard-headed Dad accepts the fact that "Sonny" is now an adult and must make decisions on his own if the business is to survive.

The Making of a Playboy

In the Martin family, carefree Rick has solved the domineering father problem by practicing avoidance. He shows up for brunch and has fond feelings for all the family, but he leaves town when too many demands fall his way.

As Robert says, "Is this a way for a grown man to act?" Rick has taken the easy way out and extended his adolescence long past its time. He doesn't get migraine headaches, and he doesn't allow problems with Robert to interfere with his pursuit of fun. But he's unable to sustain relationships outside the family. Among his female friends, Rick is known as "a fun guy but a real Peter Pan."

Rick avoids any situation, whether it be occupational, social, or sexual, that forces him to deliver. He's quick-witted and good with people, but he's never held a job that demanded more than superficial competence. And when a love affair gets too intense, he manages to float off.

Daddy's Little Girl

An adult child with a powerful parent can enjoy her father's strength and full-time involvement in life as long as she has cut that silver cord.

Most of us emancipated ourselves emotionally from our parents at the appropriate time, in adolescence or early adulthood. In that rite of passage, we left behind our dependence on our parents.

But if we didn't make the break then, we tend to get stuck in adolescence—unsure, dependent, lacking confidence as we round the corner into our own late middle age. Kathy, Robert Martin's daughter, still depends on ever-bountiful Daddy to take care of her and make the bad things go away. She genuinely loves her gentle husband, Mark, but when the chips are down, she calls Daddy. As long as her father is alive, she enjoys all the benefits of the status-quo family structure—two adoring men rushing to protect and satisfy the princess.

Still firmly attached to Robert by the silver cord, Kathy's *modus operandi* is to please her father, to manipulate him so that he shows her only adoration and protection. It never occurs to her to recognize his downright feistiness. That kind of behavior would require her to relate to Dad as a fellow adult. She just wants her father to go on being her Big Daddy forever.

In another way, her older brother, Elliott, is still stuck in adolescence. He, too, wants to please his father, and he does a lot of complicated maneuvering to keep from fighting with him. Over the years, Elliott has learned to watch his words, to avoid subjects that will displease Dad. He's still playing his father's game. Though Elliott is in his sixties, he has not yet cut that silver cord. While Kathy thrives on the status-quo relationship, Elliott's connection to his father makes him very unhappy and forces him to repress his ambitions.

The Emancipation Proclamation

Sometimes Daddy's Little Girl wakes up around age forty and wages a full-scale adolescent rebellion against her domineering parent. She begins rocking the boat, and the status-quo starts to shake a bit.

It's discomfiting for everyone to watch her thrash around and throw accusations at the parent. Tearful encounters are now commonplace. Quite often her delayed adolescent rebellion is tied up with that mid-life panic we all feel: "You mean this is all there is?"

She wants to right the wrongs that she feels were done to her in the past. She wants to grab hold of her own destiny and make deep changes. As confused as she is during such a mid-life crisis, the parent is more confused—"What's got into her? She never used to act this way."

Andrea Morris, "floating somewhere in her forties" as she expresses it, is having a dramatic mid-life crisis. After carefully selecting a domineering husband who does everything but choose her clothing for her, she is now rebelling against her whole way of life. She says it started, "When I felt the chill wind of 50 coming my way. I began to question my life. My neighbor was heavily involved in New

Age philosophy, and it opened my eyes to the way I've always lived. I've always been so subservient, first to my father, and now to Barry."

Her bewildered husband, Barry, says, "I didn't mind when she stopped wearing makeup and gave up expensive clothing. Believe me, it was a relief not to worry about all those bills. But then she got into this women's support group, and she started yelling at my father-in-law, who always adored and spoiled her. Once she went so far as to call him a 'male chauvinist.' Okay, so he's a little rough around the edges. Joe's a self-made man. I like him. He's a lot like me. But to call the poor old guy names just because he tells her what he thinks!"

Andrea is actually quite pleased with the family stir. She watches her husband and her father joining forces in their attempts to "get her back to normal," and she finds herself understanding what other girls used to talk about when she was 15. She never remembers resenting her domineering father. He gave her whatever she wanted and practically put her on a throne. Why resent all that good stuff?

But now? Andrea says, "I'm moving forward, and I'll never go back. Dad and Barry will just have to accept me. Next year I'm going to try to go to India. And if Barry won't pay for it, I'll sell my fur coat."

Men act up in mid-life, too. Quite often it's Mommy's Little Boy who lets his halo slip when the "chill wind of 50" starts to blow. He's always been a good boy. He's done all the right things—made his parents proud, married the right girl, provided a good home for his family. But if he's been following the script demanded by an overbearing parent (or parents) and he failed to emancipate himself during adolescence or early twenties, he may become one of those embarrassing middle-aged men who makes passes at the young girls in the office. "I've been a good boy," he tells himself. "Now it's my turn to have fun!"

There's something pathetic and ludicrous about adults acting out adolescent rebellion, even though their need for independence is often justified. Making the break from a demanding, domineering parent is fine, but do it in an adult way. Tilting at windmills and picking at old family sores doesn't help one cope with this kind of parent.

We need to step back, look at our status-quo situation, and stop fighting. When we have a domineering parent, we must realize that he will not easily give up his fiefdom. We can't beat him at the game of "Who's the Boss?" and we shouldn't try. Bossy Dad is not going to turn into a passive pussycat. He's going to continue to call the shots.

The question is whether we have to allow him to control our lives. When Dad tells us how to live, we have two choices: we can risk his anger and displeasure (something we should have tried twenty or thirty years ago) and assert our own rights. Or we can tune him out. The objective in both cases is the same: to run our own little world the way we wish. But rebelling against Dad at this late date only creates pain and aggravation. It's better to accept Dad's need to be the Big Shot. Continue to treat him with respect, go to the power brunch, eat the meal, and then go on to live your own grown-up life. Becoming your own person is the best revenge!

For some of us, daughters particularly, it feels so uncomfortable to "talk back" to our aging parent that we let Mom push us around. After all, she is our "elder," and when we were growing up, talking back to one's elders—our teachers, our parents' friends, our parents, our older relatives—was almost a cardinal sin.

We're often unable to risk a parent's displeasure and anger, so we suffer. We need to know that it's okay to stick up for ourselves. It's not easy. If we've been cushioned all these years by the safety net of Dad's or Mom's over-protectiveness, how do we learn to fly now?

When the safety net disappears we're vulnerable to falls. Adult children who never tried to fly during adolescence, when the time was ripe, have trouble getting their wings to work.

When a domineering parent is interfering with your life and you don't know how to handle it, you may wish to join one of the support groups in your area for adult children of aging parents. In the group environment you'll find many other people with similar problems—successful grown men and women reduced to tears and adolescent temper tantrums by their elderly parents. Or you may benefit more from individual counselling with a psychotherapist. In a later chapter, we've listed some sources that can help you make a decision.

In this chapter we have looked at the various kinds of family relationships based on status. The ideal, of course, is status-equality, with its harmonious give-and-take and respect on both sides. We wish that we and our parents could go on forever in this pleasant state of affairs.

But the only thing certain about having aging parents is that nothing is certain. Situations change, and we might find ourselves playing the dominant role and exercising power in the family. When our parents' health and financial situation begin to go downhill, we're thrust into a new role. This is *status-reversal*. Maybe the older person can no longer drive a car or remember to eat three meals a day or take his or her medicine. In any case, he or she now needs to be cared for. Sometimes this happens when a father retires and stops earning money. He may assume a dependent role and force the adult child to take over leadership. Sometimes a mother who was a life-long care-giver becomes frail and barely able to handle the tasks of everyday life.

When our parents can't make all the decisions for their own welfare anymore and we have to take over some responsibility for their lives, the dynamics are called status-reversal. For most of us, status-reversal is a difficult transition, one that we'd really rather not face. But sometimes we must face it, and in the next chapter we'll talk about techniques for getting both our parents and ourselves through this period.

Who's The Boss?

Most of our parents really do want to remain independent throughout their lives. Their biggest fear is that they will live long enough to be a burden to their children.

But as the American life span lengthens, adult "children"— sometimes as old as 75 years of age—find themselves struggling to care for the surviving members of the preceding generation. It's a fact of life: our parents, when they can no longer handle all the responsibilities of managing their own lives, become our charge, our "burden." And with this change comes a status-conflict situation. Our parents have a hard time letting go of a lifetime pattern.

The Signs Are There; You Just Have to Read Them

If we're sensitive, we can pick up on signs of a forthcoming *status-reversal* in time to pave the way for an orderly, respectful transfer of dominion.

Before our parents become dramatically dependent, there are signs that they need help. Sometimes they begin to neglect things. One daughter visited her retired bookkeeper father and was shocked to find bills stuffed in a kitchen drawer. Another daughter, investigating her mother's complaints that "the bank is making mistakes on my statement," discovered that her mother was not subtracting half her checks.

Some older people simply stop eating. Or they wear the same soiled shirt and tie for two weeks in a row. The signs are there.

If we're lucky, our offer to help with some of the tasks of daily living is accepted with a sigh of relief. Our parents hand over power to us in reasonable, adult ways, born out of a realization that they just can't handle it all anymore. They take our help graciously, and we get the feeling that they've been hoping we'd catch on and take steps to help them. In these families, status-reversal is not the painful, tumultuous process that ages us before our time.

Making a Smooth Transition

Status-reversal is easiest when we accept the painful fact that our parent's dependence is appropriate for him or her at this point in life. He is no longer able to function independently. He has passed to a new stage and has transferred some of his power to us. It's now our turn to take care of him. We also have to remember how much pain it causes him to turn over responsibilities to us.

When status-reversal occurs, we have to assume a new stance *vis-à-vis* our parents. We can't wave a magic wand and restore them to their former youth and vigor. But we don't have to remain helpless, trapped in our parents' changed circumstances.

We can teach our parents to become *competently dependent*.

We can support failing powers and still form a partnership with them. We can offer to share in their lives without stripping them of dignity. As *equals* we can help them through this transition.

If Mom can't walk to the grocery store, we can offer to shop or suggest that she phone in her order and have it delivered. If she can't see to pay her bills, we can take over the check-writing in such a way that she knows we're backing her up, assisting her as she goes about her daily chores. We're not taking everything away from her; rather, we're supplementing.

We can help our parent turn over responsibility to us by suggesting how we can work cooperatively. "I want to help. Which chores can I do? What would you like me to do?"

This makes it possible for our parents to remain competent over a long period of time. When we help them with the little details of life, it allows them to stay in control. That's the best gift we can give them.

For our aged parents, the transition to partial or complete dependence on us can be filled with anxiety and doubt. They feel dislocated, out of place, and shaky about their self-worth.

Older people who are able to transfer responsibilities to the younger generation in an open, sharing spirit have made the transition to the next step. They can turn over power without feeling threatened. They are able to give up the traditional parental role at the appropriate time and yet maintain their status. When our parent is secure about himself, his place, his goals—when he accepts his advancing age—he sees our "taking over" as the next step in the natural order of life. But when he is beset with anxieties about himself, or if we try to wrest power from him, we run into trouble!

Who's the Boss?

Older people who can't transfer their power gracefully, slowly giving over tasks and decisions to their children, are in *status-conflict*. They're holding on for all they're worth while we're trying to "help" by taking over some of the tasks they can no longer handle.

This is the most difficult time for all of us. It's a fluid period in which none of the old rules seems to apply. Warily, we circle around our parents, trying to be helpful and supportive. And just as warily, they eye our efforts, wondering if we're trying to take away their rights.

Who's the boss? Nobody is quite sure, but we spend a good deal of psychic energy jockeying for position within the family. In a strange turn of events, we find ourselves arguing with them because we love them. We want what's best for them, and we try to make them see our point of view.

Edmund Jackson says, "I was always so respectful of my parents. My Dad was a railroad porter who ran our home with a lot of pride and dignity. And when Dad was gone on a two-week run, Mama took over with the same rules. I'm proud of them and how they raised us.

"So it's been hard for me to understand why I'm fighting so much with Dad now. He lives with my sister Evelyn, and he gives her a hard time—won't do what the doctor tells him. Evelyn calls me to try to talk some sense into him. But it's not working.

"I was so ashamed last week when we all went over to Evelyn's for Sunday dinner, and I got into an argument with Dad. He's wearing these old rundown shoes that I know are going to make him trip and fall one of these days. And he won't even tie the laces. I told Dad we were going out for new shoes; he got balky and one word led to another. By the time we left, I was pretty impatient with him. My ten-year-old said to me, 'Daddy, why are you so mean to Grandpa? He can't help being old. You don't try to understand Grandpa. You're always trying to get your own way.'

"You can imagine how her words made me feel! I keep thinking, 'What's happening to me? I used to be such a nice guy and a loving son.'"

Edmund and his Dad are caught in a classic status-conflict situation. Ironically, out of his great love for his father, Edmund sees himself turning into a "bad guy."

What can Edmund do to return his relationship with his father to one of mutual respect? As difficult as it is, he has to stop badgering and nagging. The more he insists, the more his proud father will act like a crusty old curmudgeon.

Edmund's Dad may feel that all he has left is the ability to be cantankerous.

Edmund has to *circumvent* the cranky behavior—start relating to the "real" father underneath. He needs to approach each issue as if he and Dad were working out a problem: "Listen, Dad, those shoes may be comfortable but they don't support your feet. You don't want to fall and break a hip. I know how independent you are and how you'd hate being disabled. So what do you want to do? Shall we go down to the shoe store on Saturday, or should I pick out a few pair in your size and bring them around?" In this way, Edmund is offering his father a choice, still keeping him in the driver's seat, letting him make the decision and save face. But he's also letting Dad know that the issue of new shoes is not negotiable.

Jockeying for Position—When You're Trying to Be Right

Gary Shore, 50, is a successful lawyer and the only child of a "difficult," widowed mother. Stella spent her married life arguing and bickering with Gary's father while she praised their son to the skies.

Like any dutiful son, Gary basked in his mother's unqualified admiration. Until he committed the unpardonable sin—he got divorced.

Ever since he and his wife dissolved their marriage, he's been subject to his mother's criticisms and abuse. Stella informs him, "You can't even keep a marriage together. So how can you tell me what to do? I'm smarter than you, with all your education!"

Gary is beginning to pity his late father and to understand the man's evasiveness. He remembers now how Dad would stay late at the office and find reasons to go down to work on Saturdays.

He cares deeply for his mother, but she's beginning to have an effect on his nerves. He wakes at 4 A.M. for no particular reason, heart pounding, sheets damp with perspiration.

Gary sees that Stella cannot manage her own care. She has severe hypertension and must stick to a low-sodium diet. He has taken to checking her refrigerator and food cabinets for offending foods. One day he finds salted peanuts, a jar of pickles, and several bags of potato chips in the kitchen—all open and obviously half-eaten.

"What's this?" he cries dramatically, holding up an almost empty bag of chips. "Mom, this stuff is poison!"

Stella, who has never been known for docility, yells at him—"Don't you tell me what to do!"

Her son sees that either he must move Stella into his bachelor apartment or he must hire a companion who will cook and monitor his mother's food and medicine.

The companion then becomes the focus of their arguments. "I hate her. She steals all my food!" Stella says to her son, often in the companion's hearing.

She fires the companion. He hires another one. She fires that one. And so it goes.

Finally, through one of her friends, Stella finds a Polish immigrant woman who needs a job. The two women seem to get along well with sign language and a few phrases of fractured English.

Gary now sleeps through the night. He has taught the companion to use only the groceries he brings and not to let his mother buy salted snacks at the nearby drugstore.

Then, because Stella is Stella, she fires the companion, saying, "She's a nice woman, but it's getting too hard for me to cook for her." And Gary learns that his mother has been doing all the cooking!

His first impulse is to find yet another helper, one who's fluent in English. But his mother *likes* the Polish lady. So he renegotiates (what else would a good lawyer do?) and makes it known that the companion must do the cooking.

All is not perfect. But at least Stella feels she's had input in the decision and is still somewhat in charge of herself. And as she learns to accept the fact that she needs help, she's less critical of her son. In fact, during his last visit she never once mentioned his divorce—a milestone.

How could Gary have eased Stella's transition? How could he have helped her to become competently dependent? Unwittingly, he fed the flames of her burning discontent by not consulting with her. He could have held to his hidden agenda, hiring a woman to administer his mother's medicine and see to her welfare. But he also needed to help Stella hold onto her considerable pride. Consider how much easier it would have been with one of these approaches:

Gary: "Mom, I know how independent you like to be. And I see how much time you have to devote to worrying about your medication and fixing meals. It doesn't give you any time to enjoy the things you like to do. You've worked hard all your life. Now it's your turn to relax. You've earned it. Why don't you ask around among your friends and see if you can find somebody to help you in the house."

Or, "I've found some phone numbers of people who can help you. But you're the one who has to be satisfied. So you interview them and select the one you feel will be the best company."

Or, "Mom, with a little help you can still be independent, still be in charge of your life. So please allow me to do this for you. You took care of me and supported me when I needed you. Now it's my turn to help you out a little. So humor me, please!"

Or, "Mom, I'm being selfish about this. I worry too much about your medication. Let's you and I pick somebody to help you out here. I'll be able to sleep better at night. You'd be doing me an enormous favor, Mom, by putting my mind at rest."

The key is to use those good, encouraging ego-syntonic words. It requires insight and sensitivity to find creative ways to help our parents make the transition gracefully, with a minimum of aggravation for both of us.

Sometimes our parents begin behaving like children, and we're thrust into a new, unwanted role. As one outspoken 50-year-old high school teacher puts it, "I thought I'd go back to college for post-graduate work now that the kids are on their own. Instead, I go to classes on how to deal with Alzheimer's."

When Our Parents Behave Like Children

In the status-reversal situation, our parent is now the *dependent* one in the family. And because she is dependent upon us, due to her diminished physical and mental capacities, she *may behave in dependent, childlike ways*. She may begin to use the coping techniques she employed in childhood.

The dependent mother needs care now. It's at this stage that our understanding and love become paramount. It's very important to keep in mind that Mom is not acting like an unhappy child because she wants to make us miserable. She simply doesn't know how to behave differently as she watches her powers slip away.

"Sometimes I think Mom's exaggerating her weakness for my benefit," says Fred. "My mother was always an enthusiast. When she was in amateur theatrics, she went around like Sarah Bernhardt. When she took up ceramics, she flooded the house with funny-shaped ashtrays. Now that she's slowed down, I think she's really getting into manipulating me through her weakness. God save me from the tyranny of the weak!"

When Mom or Dad starts "acting like a baby," we're bewildered, frightened, angry, embarrassed. We simply don't know what to do. Our first reaction is shock: "That's my father having a temper tantrum in the hospital? I can't believe it." Next, because we're social beings, we're embarrassed by the pouts, the tantrums, the tears: "What will people think of Dad?" And our next question is, inevitably: "How will I handle this? What do I do now?"

We lie in bed at night playing out the scene we had today with Dad. Our quiet, gentlemanly father disappeared today and was replaced by a naughty, difficult six-year-old boy.

Ellis Overland was an elegant, well-spoken man who maintained a discreet distance from his children. After he retired from his job as a furniture salesman, he and his wife bought a mobile home. They lived quietly and frugally until his wife, Letitia, became ill with multiple sclerosis, and then their well-ordered life was blown apart. Her three-year illness drained Ellis, both emotionally and financially. Her expensive care practically depleted his savings, so that by the time Letitia died, Ellis was in a difficult financial position.

It was unthinkable to ask his children for help, and he certainly would not ask for government assistance. He had a position and standing in the community to maintain! So he cut corners the best he could and hoped he'd die before he needed long-term care.

When Ellis was hospitalized with heart disease compounded by poor nutrition (all those months of bad eating), he felt he'd come to the end of his rope. He'd have to let his children help him, and the thought galled him.

When his daughter Maggie, 44, went to see him Monday morning, he immediately picked a fight. "And where have you been? I've been waiting for you all morning."

"Visiting hours aren't until eleven, Dad. And I have to run over on my lunch hour. You know that."

"Bunch of foolishness. A woman working. You ought to be home taking care of your house."

"Well, I like to work," Maggie said, hoping she sounded tactful but firm. He certainly wasn't acting like her father. Mild-mannered Ellis had never criticized her before.

When it was time to leave, Ellis waved his hand. "Go on. Get going. You're always in a hurry where I'm concerned. Never do have any time for me."

His daughter heard this but couldn't believe he had said it. Just then, the nurse walked in with Ellis' medicine. Ellis set his lips and shook his head. "I won't take it."

"Oh, come on, now, Mr. Overland. You know this is good for you. You want to get well, don't you?"

"No, I don't. What for? Nobody gives a damn about me, anyway."

Maggie was so surprised she felt a nervous giggle rise in her throat.

Then, driving back to work, she thought over Ellis' performance, and she began to get angry. How dare he? She'd been a good daughter, only getting as close as he'd let her. She'd played by his rules all these years, and now he had the nerve to imply she'd been neglect-ful! Well, she'd show him. She wouldn't rush over to the hospital dur-ing lunch hour tomorrow.

It's difficult when our parents act in immature ways. We're thrown into a new script with no rehearsal and not the faintest idea of how to handle this dismaying turn of events. It's so alien to our life-long pattern that something in us closes down. We find ourselves rejecting our parents, turning away. At the same time, our heart goes out to them as we see them slip.

And we feel guilty. Mom may be crying and suffering as she loses ground, but we suffer too—thumping hearts, twisted stomachs, in-somnia, cold sweats—all the standard anxiety reactions. When Mom lists all her ailments, we feel like yelling, "You ain't heard nothin' yet!" We think of how we twisted and turned until 3:30 A.M. this morning.

We begin to get angry, just like Maggie. Our anger, born of a sense of defeat and helplessness, is self-righteous: "I've done so much for him. How can he treat me this way?" During those sleepless nights we make lists: "I took him to the doctor. I made him a nice beef stew. I did his laundry. I refilled his prescription." And on and on. Pretty soon, we're behaving as childishly as our aging parent.

Help! I Forgot to Get a Transfer!

The transfer of dominion from parent to child can be made smooth-ly or it can be a hotbed of bad feelings on both sides. We've dis-cussed some of the problems that arise when our parents are unwilling to let go. But remember, status-reversal is a two-way street. Adult children have a wealth of problems of their own when it comes to changing the family power structure. The more aware we are of our own feelings, the better able we are to cope with our fami-ly dynamics.

Many of us are reluctant to face the fact that our parents are ag-ing. We still want to please—and can't let go of the all-powerful par-ent of our childhood. The way we act with our parents has been "set in stone" by our childhood roles. Almost comically, we hang back as our parents age, thinking, "What right do I have to make decisions for my mother?" Our automatic tendency is to see them as authorities, and it's hard to get over that. Often we don't even know that we're having trouble effecting a transfer. We only know that something is making us uneasy, guilty, and angry.

Carolyn Riley suffers from the "Wait, Mom, I'm not ready" syndrome. She is unwilling to carry out her part of the transfer. She refuses the assignment. "I feel so awful when my mother turns to me in the doctor's office and says, 'You talk to him. You'll understand what he's saying.' It's as if I'm talking over the head of my four-year-old grandson. I find myself wishing my mother would be the person she used to be. I just don't know how to handle this," she says.

It's My Turn Now

"Taking over" is hard to do.

When our parent's status begins changing, we're thrown for a loop. How much do we do? And when? How do we talk about it? How do we help in an appropriate way without hurting Mom or Dad?

All of us fervently hope that our parents are lucky enough to be active and vital to the end of their lives. It's painful to think that we might have to "take over." The possibility taps into our deepest conflicting feelings. We don't want to be their keepers. We don't feel "right" about taking away any of their power and control.

The "Peter Pan" in all of us resists. Taking an active role in caring for our parents marks a new rite of passage. We're not kids any more! This is grown-up stuff. Are we ready for this? We tell ourselves that tomorrow Mom will be her old self again. We delude ourselves with comfortable rationalizations that we've perfected through the years.

We avoid the inevitable.

Deny, Deny, Deny

Some of us have such trouble accepting the changes in our parents that we construct an unreal situation in which Mom is still completely in control. In reality, she needs help.

She is so busy pretending to be in charge and guarding her autonomy that she is virtually incapable of asking for assistance. And we're so involved in supporting the fantasy that we refuse to see the real situation.

Irma Hansen, 76, has been an active, lively woman her whole life. Just six years ago, she drove her car from her home in Baltimore to Toledo, Ohio, to visit her son and his family.

Irma is one of those women who has never given her children a moment of anxiety. She's lived alone for more than thirty years, since "Pa" died. Her children have treated Irma with a kind of benign neglect.

But recently, son Carl has been getting phone calls from the police in Baltimore. "Your mother shouldn't be driving, Mr. Hansen. She goes to a new neighborhood and gets lost. We found her wandering around down near the docks last week, and she couldn't remember where she parked the car."

Carl is incredulous: "You sure you're talking about my mother? She's sharp as a tack." Carl is very proud of his independent mother and grateful that she demands so little of him.

"Yes, we're sure—I found your number in her wallet. She couldn't think of your street address or the town you live in. I think you better look into it. Has she been ill recently?"

Carl and his wife are shocked and more than a little embarrassed that Irma is behaving in such a bizarre manner. He decides to say nothing about it to his mother but to arrange that his aunt Mathilde, the "baby of the family," age 72, keep an eye on Irma.

The situation goes on for several months. Carl gets phone calls more often now. Aunt Mathilde finally calls and tries to talk to Carl between bouts of crying. "I'm so worried. She's not herself. She's thin as a rail, and she's taken to staying in her house all the time."

Carl is busy at work and he just can't spare the time to run up to Baltimore, not with a promotion in the offing.

A few weeks later, his Aunt Mathilde calls once more. "Your mother is in the hospital."

"Hospital? Ma's strong. She's never sick! What is it? Flu?"

"No, your mother is suffering from malnutrition, the doctor says. And he's giving her brain tests. He's not sure whether she's confused from lack of proper food or what it is."

"Should I come there?" he asks.

Quiet Aunt Mathilde sounds downright testy. "Well, I should think you'd want to," she says and hangs up.

Carl is positive Aunt Mathilde is overreacting. Irma's a strong woman. She'll be herself again soon—she's just going through a rough patch.

But he flies to Baltimore to see for himself. Carl is greeted by Irma's doctor, a geriatric psychiatrist, and the hospital social worker. They all have the same accusing look on their faces, it seems to him. And they all say the same thing. "You'll have to make a decision here, Mr. Hansen. Your mother can't live alone any more."

Quite often we need a graphic demonstration such as this one to show us the light. We're forced into facing our parent's debility, whether we like it or not.

When our parents need to turn over their power and authority to us and we persistently behave like ostriches, we're denying not only the change in our parents but the grim possibility of *our own mortality.* When they die and go away, we're next on the list! It is not surprising that we act like Carl, squirming and avoiding the truth. The truth hurts.

When we stop dealing with the parent-child relationship the way we always knew it, and say—"I'm the adult now. I have the authority and I'll deal with what needs to be done. I want to help. I want to do what is best for my parent"—we've reached maturity. It takes some of us longer to get there. But because most of us really do love our parents and want to fulfill our obligations, we finally make it.

The Power of Water Power

In an unresolved conflict relationship, often our parents are ambivalent. They want to maintain their status and what they view as their rightful place in the family, but they'd like to get rid of some responsibilities, too. So they send us mixed messages, sometimes so convoluted that we miss the whole point.

Eighty-year-old Wanda Schurr, whose eyesight is failing, refuses any household help. Her daughter Valerie is appalled by the spilled food that Mother can't see, the dust motes piling up under the TV. In her prime, Wanda was a fastidious housekeeper and took great pride in her home.

One Sunday Valerie shows up unannounced with a mop and cleaning supplies. "I can't stand this mess, Mom. It will take me all afternoon to clean it up."

Later that night, a tearful Valerie tells her husband about Wanda's reaction. "She nearly threw me out. The minute she saw the mop she burst into tears and cried and harangued for hours. 'Who are *you* to tell me how to clean house?' By the time I left, the house was still dirty and I was a basket case."

Wanda is holding onto her dominion, her little kingdom, for dear life. Though she knows she can't see well enough to maintain her household, she resolutely clings to her front. She construes Valerie's offers of help as a plot to take over her life. In this case the mop becomes a bitterly contested symbol of Mother's status.

Valerie says, "I freely admit I'm a coward. I can't stand the tears and arguing, so I retreat every time. I figure when Mom gets sick and goes to the hospital, I'll go in there with a cleaning lady and put her place in shape. I just don't know what else to do."

Valerie is having problems taking the reins, so she lets her mother control her with "water power." By responding to her mother's bullying tactics and copious tears and not the real need to help her mother, she is avoiding the real issue.

Valerie could have enlisted her mother's cooperation by first discussing the problem—tactfully and by using ego-syntonic language. In this way she could build up a cooperative venture, a partnership of two equals working on a project, instead of a power struggle.

Parents who are struggling with their own failing powers often engage us in arguments we can't win. The minute we succumb and fight over the house cleaning, trying to justify our actions, we're in trouble. In this case, Valerie should have refused to fight. She had no need to prove the rightness of her cause. The house was dirty and Wanda couldn't handle it. But the job had to be done. Valerie, afraid of hurting Wanda's feelings, backed off the issue. When we start worrying about what mother thinks of what we're doing, we're lost.

We also must deal with unnecessary guilt. If we help, we're not doing anything wrong! The key is to help cooperatively, kindly, and to make sure our parent is an active participant, not a helpless pawn.

Revenge Is Not So Sweet

At the other end of the spectrum from Valerie is the power-hungry child. Such a person takes advantage of a parent's failing powers to seek revenge for an unpleasant or painful childhood. Our powerful parent may have given us a sense of helplessness; he may have walked all over our feelings. We swore that someday we'd get back at him, and now we can! If we're trying to wrest power before it's time for it to be freely given over, we need to sit back and examine our motives honestly. Are we getting a charge out of finally being in charge? Are we so busy building own bossy little domain that we're prematurely taking away all the power from our elderly parent and stripping him of dignity?

Nothing I Do Is Ever Enough!

With some parents, service on demand has been expected of us from the day we climbed over the rail of our playpen. Parents with demanding personalities rarely get better as they age! As we move into the "space" they've carefully cordoned off, they become irate. How dare we try to seize power?

Felice Terman, 51, is a widowed third-grade teacher with an active life. She spends a lot of time participating in advanced seminars and counseling the parents of "problem kids," with whom she has a special rapport. Her handsome husband died of a heart attack earlier this year.

Felice says, "I always thought I could handle anything. When Bill died I had to grapple with a hundred new problems and deal with my grief, too. I've gone through my three kids' adolescence and my daughter's divorce. But my father is the last straw. He's always angry at me. Whenever I visit him, I leave with a massive, pounding headache."

Felice's father, Henry, has been a domineering, demanding person throughout his life. The only son in a family of seven children, Henry learned early in life to make noise to get what he wanted.

He lives alone in a retirement hotel in the north suburbs of Chicago. When Bill died, Henry suggested that he move in with Felice. Felice refused. She simply wasn't ready. Henry can't understand it;

Felice has always done everything he expected of her. Suddenly she's acting so distant.

Felice says Dad's inordinate demands are wearing her down. "I almost feel as though Dad is punishing me because I didn't ask him to move into my house. He needs a lot of attention, and I just don't feel emotionally able to give any more than I do right now. If he lived with me, I'd have to give up everything and rush right home from school every day. I can't do it. Right now, he calls me three or four times a day, always demanding that I drive down to Evanston immediately. It takes me 30 minutes to get there as it is, but I try to make it two or three times a week. It's not enough for him. He's always complaining."

The usual scenario involves Felice driving from her home to the retirement hotel in rush-hour traffic. She arrives there with a bag of items Henry has requested. He keeps her waiting for five minutes while he pretends not to hear her at the door.

Finally, he opens the door very slowly and peers around the door frame. "Oh, are you someone I know?" he says to his daughter.

"Yup. Just me, Dad."

"Really? Is that really my daughter? It's been so long since I've seen you, I forgot what you look like."

Felice smiles wearily. "Dad, I was here Tuesday."

"So, big deal. You spend five minutes and run. I never know when you're here. You don't stay long enough. I get more conversation from the desk clerk in this hotel."

Felice unpacks Henry's clean laundry. "Here, Dad, here's your washing. Want me to put it away?"

Henry shrugs. "Do whatever you want."

Felice puts away the laundry and sorts through the chest of drawers for dirty clothes. No matter how she begs him not to, Henry persists in storing dirty clothes with clean items; she goes through this procedure twice a week.

Henry says, "I don't suppose you'll have time to take me out on Saturday. I've been stuck in here all week."

"Didn't you go out for lunch with the Men's Club yesterday?"

"Sure, but I didn't like it. I like to drive out in the suburbs where my fancy daughter lives and see all the trees. Here I've got concrete and papers blowing around. What's so nice about that?"

"Dad, I have root canal work scheduled for this Saturday."

"You have time for everyone but me," Henry says with great bitterness.

Felice is knocking herself out trying to please her father, and nothing is working. The more she does for him, the more he demands. Henry is more than willing to have Felice run around doing the "dirty work," but he continues to treat her like a slightly backward servant.

As he keeps her waiting in the hall, he's sending her a multifaceted message through the closed door. "I'm in control here. I'm the parent and I have authority over you. As long as you persist in denying me my rightful place in your home, I'll make you see how difficult it is when we maintain two households."

The domineering, demanding parent like Henry never feels his child is doing enough. By his words and actions he reminds us of "all I did for you when you were growing up; this is the least you can do for me."

He finds the mother lode of our guilt and mines it unmercifully.

The demanding parent manufactures conflicts out of thin air.

We have to learn how to "save ourselves," withdraw from the conflict yet still help. All of us want to be "good" sons and daughters, but we don't have to be doormats. When Dad's demands represent attempts to control, we don't have to give in. In the most loving but firm way, we must delineate between what we can and cannot do.

Felice is caught up in her father's manipulations. She allows Henry to keep her waiting in the hall and to harass her during the entire visit. She wouldn't let one of her third-graders push her around in that manner, nor would she allow a fellow teacher to play such control games. When she stops feeling so guilty and starts seeing her father as an aging, frustrated human being, she can react to his unreasonable demands in a realistic way. She can say, "No."

They're Only Human

We can't say it often enough: the misunderstandings and missed connections between us and our aging parents are rooted in our inability to see each other as human beings. There's more to each of us than the roles we've always played for one another.

If we don't recast each other as something—or someone—besides "parent" and "child," we can't view each other as fellow human beings. We're able to summon huge reservoirs of understanding and insight for our friends, but it's hard to see the *person* in the parent. Only if we do so, however, can we identify and meet our parent's real needs.

Anita Ehrlich, 47, came from a difficult family. Her German father, Otto, was the strong know-it-all who protected Anita's mother, whom he called his "little Dresden doll."

The "doll" was born into a prosperous Southern family who taught her how to play the piano, to dress well, to make proper conversation, and not to get her hands either wet or dirty. Anita was reared almost exclusively by a series of maids.

When Otto reached his eighties, he began to act oddly, making phone calls in the middle of the night, rising at 4 A.M. and dressing to go to his office, starting bitter arguments with grocery clerks and the elevator operator in their old but elegant New York apartment building.

Anita has never discussed "real" issues with her mother, but she sees that something must be done: "Mother, what do you think is wrong with Dad?"

"What do you mean? I don't see anything unusual." Lenora immediately picks up her embroidery and begins talking about the weather.

"Something's wrong. Mrs. Polanski in the deli told me that he goes in there and fights with everyone. And the maid said he gets up before dawn and tries to go to work."

Lenora shakes her head. "Well, he seems about the same to me."

So much for her mother's awareness of reality.

Otto deteriorates rapidly until Anita seeks psychiatric help to learn how to deal with him. He's now quite paranoid and makes life miserable for everyone, even jolting her mother out of her fog.

Anita tries to enlist her mother's aid, but Lenora confines her activity to wringing her hands and retiring to her bedroom with a cold cloth on her head.

Always somewhat distant from her parents, Anita is now heavily embroiled in dealing with Otto. Shouting matches become normal as she insists on handling the checkbook.

Otto, a life-long male chauvinist, says, "You're only a woman. What do you know about financial matters?"

Finally, Anita enlists the aid of the maid, who spirits the check-book out of Otto's desk. When Anita looks at the balance, she sees an alarming number of $1,000 checks made out to "Cash" and various stock brokers.

Desperately she tries to convince Otto to see the psychiatrist. He rants and raves and clings to his rights and his rightful status: "I'm the father here," he shouts every time she makes a decision for her parents.

As Otto grows more demented and Lenora refuses to take any responsibility, Anita says, "I've had to grow up. There's nobody to do things for them. It has to be me. It's been hard because neither of them were loving parents. My father just wanted obedience, and my mother was never really 'there.' A dozen times I've asked myself, 'Why me?' But I know the answer. No matter how much they hurt me when I was growing up, they need me now, and I can't turn my back on them."

A Topsy-Turvy World

When our parent enters status-reversal, it's as if we're both living in an upside-down world. The guidelines we and our parents took for granted are now in flux. It takes our time, our patience, and our commitment to adjust to this new stage of life. We need to accept what has happened as a natural step in the aging process. And we must forgive ourselves for the difficulties we have in dealing with the turn of events. This is a stressful time for our parents and for us. This is brand-new territory. We have to restructure life-long roles and begin to handle problems we never had to face before. But if we try, by working together with our parents, we can come through this difficult time together.

Breaking Out of Old, Destructive Patterns

Too often, our relationships with our aging parents are set in patterns that are destructive for everyone. Mom, trying to hold on to her status, does things that upset and baffle us. Her behavior makes us feel terrible. We "buy into" the system and react in ways that reinforce her misbehavior. She continues to push our buttons. We react again, *ad infinitum*.

In this chapter we'll discuss ways to break out of that vicious cycle and begin to form new, more constructive relationships with our parents.

Our Feelings Are the Clue to Our Parents' Motives

The first step in building better relationships with our parents is to understand what motivates their misbehavior. The secret is simple: *the anger, guilt, frustration, and confusion we feel are what our parent wants to make us feel* although they themselves may be unaware of their motives. If we are able to discover these underlying motives, we can begin to develop more appropriate responses—responses that meet his or her real needs instead of reinforcing bad behavior.

Unfortunately, our parent's underlying motive or goal doesn't conveniently sport a little sign that says, "This is it." We have to reason it out, starting with the way we feel.

71

The work of psychiatrists Alfred Adler and Rudolf Dreikurs helps parents to diagnose their children's bad behavior in terms of how the behavior makes the parents feel. Certainly we can't analyze our aging parent's behavior as we would that of a rambunctious two-year-old. But we can use the same techniques to understand our parent's unconscious goals and put a stop to "misbehavior" by the *way we respond.*

"All human behavior," writes Dr. Rudolf Dreikurs, "has a purpose and is a movement toward a goal.... If we want to help a child change his direction, we must understand what makes him move."

In every relationship between two or more people, there are fascinating patterns of interaction. Husbands dominate wives, wives seek revenge, adolescents play complicated games—the scenarios are endlessly varied. Everywhere we look we find intricate, long-standing patterns within families, even between friends and co-workers. These behavior patterns keep the relationship going.

As our parents age, the patterns that always existed intensify. The older person becomes more rigid and hangs on to what he knows, the methods he always used to control his environment and the people in it. Mom's effort to control us is her *goal.* Our reaction is the *payoff.*

The chart below shows three common goals of elderly parents and the reactions, or payoffs, they produce in adult children.

PARENT'S GOAL	OUR REACTION
Attention, love, service	Anxiety, worry, guilt. "Am I doing enough?" "What have I done to make her so unhappy?"
Power display to hold on to status	Frustration, sense of helplessness. "What do I do now?"
Getting even, revenge	Anger, hurt. "How could she do this to me?"

When we're upset, confused, and guilty, it doesn't help to keep blaming our parents. The only way we can change what they're doing is to *change our responses.*

We can start by analyzing what's happening in the interchange between our aging parent and us. Our thought process might go something like this:

1. This is what Mom is doing (turning on "water" power, "zinging" us, begging for attention, dumping, arguing, blaming).

2. This is what I think is behind her behavior (a need for service and attention, getting even, jockeying for position).

3. This is how I'm reacting (anger, frustration, sense of helplessness, physical symptoms).

4. How can I change it? What message do I want to send? "You make me angry but I still love you." "I'm going to stick with you no matter how mean you are to me." "I'll love you and respect you but I won't be a doormat." "I want to help you but this has to be a team effort; we'll work together.

Additional questions must be considered: What do I say? What tone of voice do I use? How should I act? If I deliver a "love message" with a scowl on my face, can it work? Will she believe my good words if the cords are standing out in my neck?

Now let's look at some specific goals of "misbehavior" and find out how we can deal with them.

Dealing with Excessive Demands for Attention, Love, and Service

Attention, love, and service interconnect. When we "wait on" our parents, fuss over them, run errands, make telephone calls, change light bulbs, bring a pound of grapes, listen to their complaints—our service represents love. Like children, elderly parents can demand more and more service. And they increasingly resent any attention we give to other facets of our own lives.

Sue Burgess, 50, is "just now climbing out of the morass of motherhood," she says. After raising five children and divorcing her husband last year, she's putting her life in order. Sue is in law school and looking forward to a strong career commitment. Two months ago her 79-year-old mother went into the hospital with a case of flu.

"It was downhill all the way after that," Sue recalls. "My mother refused to eat unless I was there. I was running from the campus to the hospital in cross-town traffic, piling up parking tickets. The nurses were delighted with the service my mother was getting from me.

Then one day I had a late exam and just couldn't get there. I walked into my mother's room two hours late, and she turned her head to the wall and wouldn't talk.

"I slunk out of there engulfed in guilt. I was so upset I found myself wishing she'd just die peacefully before she got any more difficult. I'm a religious person and found my feelings very hard to reconcile. Worse, I couldn't talk to anyone about it. I tried once to discuss it with my older son, and he got very self-righteous. 'She's an old sick lady; how can you be so selfish,' was his response."

"Mom is back in her own apartment now and calls me constantly. I'm trying my best to help her, but I really feel like I'm drowning. It's as if I can't satisfy her demands, ever. I now just hate to go there."

When Mom starts demanding more attention, we all follow a similar script. We begin by feeling concerned: "What's wrong with her? Is she getting senile?" Then we get guilt panels: "What did I do or not do to make her so demanding and angry?" Ultimately we feel defeated: "I just can't win."

Our parents don't really want to hurt us, even though they stage these confrontations. Like the four-year-old boy who jumps up and down fifty times to get us off the telephone, they're simply saying, "Look at me. Pay attention to me. Prove you love me."

There are a few techniques we can use. Try giving love and service *before* Mom resorts to provocative behavior. "Give the Lady What She Wants" was the slogan originated by the founder of Marshall Field and Co. A Field's customer got attention and kind service *before* she had to ask for it.

Jeannette Fourtier, 47, has finally discovered a technique that works with her demanding, elderly mother. Jeannette calls her mother frequently:

"Mama, where have you been? How come you didn't call me? I have been waiting here. You told me you would report on your visit to the doctor."

Mother (with hesitation): "Oh, well, I guess I just forgot."

Jeannette has answered Mom's need for attention. She has let her mother know that her welfare is important, but Jeannette has seized the initiative. She's no longer reacting with a knee-jerk guilt response. In fact, she's guiding her mother into worrying about pleasing Jeannette instead of constantly demanding attention. Jeannette has discovered the value of putting the parent back in her parental role and making her worry about her children for a change.

> Jeannette: "Oh, Mama, I wanted to come and see you last Tuesday but my back is just terrible."
>
> Mother: "What did you do to it?"
>
> Jeannette: "I was making the bed and it just snapped. A few days of rest and I know I'll be better."

Jeannette says, "I've learned that to deal with my mother I must 'top her story.' When I complain about my husband or how my children upset me or my demanding boss, I notice Mama doesn't call as much. It's not fun to talk to me when I'm clamoring for someone to hear my story. In a roundabout way, I feel I've helped my mother. I let her know I still need her attention, that she's an important part of my life. I used to ignore my own needs in our conversations. And Mother became more and more demanding, more provocative. When I was 'all ears' and rushing to keep up with her next demand, she was impossible."

We're not advocating ignoring your parent's need for attention; rather, we're suggesting you try dealing with it before it becomes excessive and a source of anger and guilt. We're suggesting that you *intervene,* interrupt the destructive, painful patterns so that both of you can relate in a more positive manner.

You can get your message across by what you say. When Mom is demanding undue attention and service, holding you emotional hostage by forcing you to prove your love over and over, you can say "No" in the most constructive manner. This is the time to enlist her cooperation: "I love you and I want to help you, but I can't do any better than this. If we work together, I know we can make things better."

One desperate woman was so overwhelmed by her mother's incessant demands for attention that one day she finally burst into tears. "I just let down my guard and let her see what she was doing to me. Amazingly, she began patting my shoulders and telling me that everything would be fine. I realized afterward that I had given my mother back her role. I had allowed her to comfort me for a change. It was a revelation for both of us. Since then, she seems to be much more aware of my needs and frustrations."

Dealing with Power Displays

Even the most frail among our aging parents are capable of impressive power performances. As they cope with their escalating losses, they hold on tightly to what's left. When we threaten their self-esteem, threaten to take away their function and role, they marshal their failing forces and give us a "double-whammy." Their goal is clearly to let us know that they still have power. They've been around longer than we, and we'd better keep that in mind.

Paul and Marcia Gilbert have always enjoyed a close, compatible relationship with Marcia's maiden aunt Rachel, now 83. Until recently, Aunt Rachel would take the bus downtown and meet them for dinner and the symphony. But in the last year her arthritis has prevented her from using public transportation.

Now they pick her up on Saturday or Sunday morning and have brunch at a nearby restaurant.

"What used to be a pleasant interlude in our busy week has turned into a nightmare," Marcia says. "The pliable, cooperative aunt I knew is rapidly turning into a tyrant. One time she made us wait forty minutes while she changed her clothes several times. Or she finds something minute to complain about—the fan is blowing too hard overhead or her chair isn't comfortable or the waiter slighted her or there's a speck in the water glass.

"Paul and I are simply baffled. We used to have stimulating conversations about the books she was reading or a program on educational television. Now all she talks about is how she told off the doctor. I actually dread these brunches now. Halfway through, I feel my stomach churn into high. We just don't know what to do. She needs us. We're all she has, but she's driving us away."

Marcia and Paul are the audience for Rachel's particular brand of power display. Rachel is losing her physical powers through debilitating arthritis. Her world and her options are shrinking, and she's compensating by clinging to whatever power she has left—even if it's something as small as making the waiter bring her a new glass of water.

What can Paul and Marcia do to improve the situation? First of all, they're already doing something constructive and loving. They've not abandoned her. They still see her, and they listen to her complaints.

Rachel lives alone and needs this opportunity to talk about her troubles.

But they don't need to remain captive to her display of power. They can structure the conversation so that all three of them are talking on an equal basis about literature, music, and other topics they have in common. After Rachel has had her chance to "vent" and they've shown her the deference she's seeking, it's time to steer the conversation away from her ailments.

Rachel can get a feeling of power, of still being in charge, from a "good goal." She can contribute and be valued for her knowledge and expertise, not her petty squabbles with people.

How to Sidestep Manipulation

It's particularly galling to have to deal with geriatric power struggles. We would like nothing more than to maintain an idealized picture of our elders as people who have the purest motives toward us. We'd rather avoid the hassles and just be with them when they're nice to us. When our Aunt Rachel begins to get on our nerves, our first reaction is to find reasons not to take her to restaurants anymore. We remove ourselves not because we're cruel and unfeeling but because we don't know what to do.

Sadly, when older people "act up" and try to gain the upper hand, they elicit the very response they least want and need— avoidance. They become cut off when they most desperately need love and companionship.

When our parent or older relative sets up a power struggle, we must remove ourselves from the manipulation—not from them. It's hard to do, but we must ignore the power display and focus on the fears and frustrations underlying the performance.

If we fly off the handle and force a confrontation, the power struggle escalates. Putting the power struggle in another context, you've seen what happens when a misbehaving child mounts a performance in the supermarket. He grabs a candy bar off the shelf. His mother slaps his hand. The child starts to wail, "I wanta candy bar!" His mother raises her voice and tries to overpower him by her "rightness" as his authority figure: "You will NOT have a candy bar because I say so!" The child yells louder, and soon the whole supermarket is in an uproar. The child has triumphed because he's upset Mother, and Mother is entertaining thoughts of finding a boarding school for four-year-olds.

Here are some tips for dealing with an elderly relative who's unconsciously trying to manipulate you through a display of power.

1) *Don't try to win.* If Dad needs so desperately to display the remnants of his power, can't we be "big" enough to let him do it?

Father: "Bought one of those foreign cars again? Bet you're having plenty of engine trouble."

Son: "No, Dad, so far, so good."

Father: "Too early to tell. You'll see. Darn thing'll just collapse one day on the road. And then where will you be?"

Son: "Guess I'll have to wait and see."

Here's a son who's learned to sidestep the manipulation. His Dad is pushing all the right buttons. They've had arguments before about the merits of imported cars, or cheese or beer, versus the "good old American things" his Dad is so partial to. His father loves to needle him, cause him to blow up and fight back. So the son has learned not to respond, not to take the bait. The son says, "Sometimes I feel a little guilty. I've deprived Dad of all the fun he used to have baiting me, pushing me until I'd yell at him. But it's certainly easier on my stomach. I know he walks away convinced he's shown me that he still knows more than I do. And that's okay. It's not important who wins."

2) *Use neutral words.* Try putting the conversation into third-person, less-emotional language: "Guess that could be so," "You may be right," "That's always a possibility," "Sure seems that way." These innocuous responses tend to defuse temper tantrums. It's not much fun to struggle with a wishy-washy opponent.

3) *Don't try to get the last word.* You're not engaged in a courtroom drama. It's not necessary to be absolutely RIGHT about everything. If Mom says something you are sure is inaccurate, the wisest course might be to let it slide.

Patricia Hernandez' mother is 83 and still considers herself the Supreme Matriarch. A mother of eight children, she wields the vestiges of her control with a strong hand.

Patricia:"Mama, where did you put the new rice I bought you?"

Mama:"What rice? You didn't bring me any rice. I certainly asked you enough times, but you never did it."

Patricia:"Last week, Mama. Last week I brought you three pounds from the Mexican grocery. Remember? It was the day I drove you to the hairdresser."

Mama (shaking head):"No. You forgot it."

Patricia:"I did not! Now where did you put it?"

Patricia is as stubborn as her mother. They could go on all day arguing about the rice. Why not just go out and buy more? The three pounds will turn up one day anyway. And Patricia could let her mother "save face." When we insist on the last word, we lose our parents' respect and rob them of some of their dignity.

You may lose all the little battles. You have to be prepared to accept that or your relationship will deteriorate to one of constant bickering, of jockeying for top position. When parents are undergoing status-conflict, we easily fall into the trap of trying to be boss. Mom is fiercely defending her sense of identity, so she'll fight us "tooth and nail" on anything that threatens it. If Mom persists in using her oven to make baked potatoes when you've spent hours explaining why she should use the microwave oven you just bought her, give up. Why is it so important to win that battle? If she's wearing a copper bracelet and is convinced that it's curing her arthritis, take the guilt-free path. Don't try to argue her out of it. Buy her a pair of copper earrings to match.

When we nag Mom about the little stuff, we're setting ourselves up for retaliation. She dislikes being nagged as much as we do, and she'll get back at us with those guilt-laden words that go straight to our weak spots.

We need to save our shots. If Mom is losing her color vision and sometimes wears clashing colors, we have to work out with her whether or not she wants us to tell her about her fashion "gaffe." If Mom says she wants us to tell her but gets angry when we suggest she change her clothes, we might consider letting her follow her own rainbow. If it's not a major social catastrophe, let the colors fall where they may. It beats useless arguing that leaves everyone feeling bad.

When It's Okay to Win

Once you've resigned yourself to losing gracefully, it doesn't mean you're totally off the hook. You still have responsibility for your parents in health and welfare issues. You still want to help them and protect them. *There are certain battles that are important for you to win.*

If, for example, Mom is forgetting to latch her door at night, you have to step in. If your nagging up to this point has not convinced her, perhaps you can arrange with her building doorman or a neighbor to check and remind her about the door latch each evening. When you arrange this kind of *cooperative effort,* Mom is more likely to agree to the door-latch project. She may not like being checked on but she'll accept the wisdom of it.

If Mom wore drop-dead glamour shoes with spike heels all her life and she's still tottering around on them despite her arthritis and poor balance, it's time to intervene. You wouldn't stand by and watch your child hurt himself, and you can't let your mother set herself up for a disastrous fall. In the most tactful way, assuring Mom that she'll still be a knockout in more sturdy shoes, you bite the bullet and take her shopping for new shoes. It won't be easy. She'll fight you all the way, but you'll have one less worry to keep you awake nights.

Bob Wagner manages an orthopedic shoe store and has learned how to deal with aging mothers and nervous daughters. He says, "I make sure I talk directly to the mother. She's the one who must be comfortable and happy with the shoes. Initially, she's always resistant. 'I won't wear old lady shoes!' But I point out that if she wants to enjoy her life and be able to walk safely, this is her solution. When the daughter stops trying to convince her mother and turns the task over to me, an objective third party, it works out fine. I've had some bad times when the mother and daughter stage a full-fledged fight in the store and try to get me to side with one or the other of them. I've learned to remain detached and still try to please the older woman who has to wear the shoes."

Let your parent know what she can reasonably expect you to do. When our four-year-old gets locked in a power struggle with us, it's because he is unsure of *what is expected.* When a child knows what behavior will be tolerated in which situation, he's not going to push beyond that limit. By the same token, when our parents are trying to engage us in a power struggle, it's up to us to set the limit, let them know where we draw the line. If things are getting out of hand, we need to say, "Enough!"

We must remember that a power struggle is only satisfying when there's an opponent. We must refuse to be that opponent; it isn't good for our aging parents, it leads to further deterioration of our relationship, and it's downright hazardous to our health.

How to Deal with A Parent's Desire for Revenge

If we sat down and wrote a list of all the reasons for getting even with the people we love the most—our parents, our mates, our children, our best friends—we could fill a book.

Unconscious revenge is a powerful motive. Our parents may want to get back at us for any one of a hundred reasons. Maybe they're angry at us for choosing the person we married. Or maybe they're disappointed in our children, who are not reflecting enough glory on them. Or perhaps they think of us as grown-up babies who are still doing the same dumb things we did as children.

They like to zap us from time to time just to show they're still in control. It's their way of demonstrating their anger and displeasure.

There's obviously no way you can change all the debits you piled up in Mom's ledger. And there's absolutely no profit in trying to discover "what you did" to make her want to pay you back. So Rule Number One for dealing with a vengeful parent is *don't try to atone for your past sins.*

Nicole Washington, 50, is a successful insurance agent—the first black woman to represent her prestigious old-line company. Years ago she divorced her charming, irresponsible husband, whose earnings went straight from his pocket to the racetrack. Single-handedly, she reared three children, who are now out of college. To the rest of the world, Nicole "has it made."

But Nicole's mother, Matilda, thinks differently. She "zings" her daughter at every visit.

Matilda: "You got so high-falutin' with that fancy job. Seems to me you let family fall by the wayside."

Nicole: "Mom, I've had to support myself and the kids all these years. What choice do I have?"

Matilda: "I told you not to marry Charles. I knew he wasn't good enough for you. You didn't listen to me, and now look at you!"'

When she's calmed down and away from her mother, Nicole sees the humor in their situation. She says, "Mother is still punishing me for a decision I made when I was 21. There's no way I can deal with it unless I go back in time warp with her. I haven't seen Charles in 17 years. I bet he'd be surprised at the impact he made on my mother."

Actually, Nicole could have handled her mother more appropriately by refusing to fall into Matilda's trap. They've had the conversation about the ex-husband countless times. The daughter knows the words "support myself and the kids" are buzz words for Matilda—the perfect opening for her opinions on a marriage she never approved. Nicole has to learn to avoid that issue—refuse to talk about it and change the subject. Which brings us to the second rule in dealing with a parent intent on revenge.

Rule Number Two is *remove the target.* When Mom is in a zinging mood, get out of the way. Arrows only hurt when they find a place to land. If we refuse to respond, our parent will be, as Dr. Dreikurs says, "A victor on an empty field." When our parent sees that her unconscious revenge behavior is failing to affect us, she'll abandon the battle.

Jack and Lisa McDonald were having such difficulties with Jack's aging mother that they consulted a therapist. Mrs. McDonald lives downstairs in an in-law apartment, and in recent years she's spent every evening visiting with them.

Lisa says, "She's really getting mean. It's as if she resents us for being younger and more active. When the phone rings, she looks at me as though I've abandoned my job as a wife and daughter-in-law. And if we go out for dinner during the week, well, do we get punished the next day!"

Jack says, "I just let her rant. I don't pay any attention to that kind of carrying on. When our kids were little, I ignored their temper tantrums. I do the same thing with my mother."

Lisa says, "That's just the trouble. When Mother starts haranguing us, Jack just picks up the newspaper."

Well done, Jack! When Mom is retaliating, pushing us beyond reasonable boundaries, we need to "tune out" temporarily—pick up a newspaper, turn on the television, read a book. Certainly we're not suggesting you ignore your parents or "tune out" to their real needs for love and attention. But when Mom is throwing barbed comments, why be the target? Jack is sending a clear message by his refusal to get involved: "I love you, Mom, but I don't have to sit still for nasty remarks."

Jack has no reason to feel guilty about his response to his mother. His only fault lies in abandoning the field and letting his wife cope alone. Most daughters and daughters-in-law complain that their husbands "just bow out and leave me in the middle of the mess." To be really effective, Jack must do more than ignore his mother's snide comments. He has to convince Lisa to join him in his passive resistance campaign. When they *both* pick up a book each time Mom goes on the warpath, Jack's mother will understand that both of them refuse to play the game.

Rule Number Three: *focus on Mom in a positive way.* You've ignored the bad behavior. Now "accentuate the positive," as the old song advises. Encourage Mom with comforting ego-syntonic words that you can expect to make her feel better. Give her a hug or two.

Remember, Mom is needling you because she's so unhappy. See if you can cheer her up a little. Remember, also, that she's aiming zingers to get a rise out of you. Surprise her! Don't respond in kind.

Bids for attention, power displays, and retaliation are three of the more common goals of misbehavior in that complex network that binds us to our parents. Most of the problems we encounter with our aging parents can be traced back to those motives.

Throwing the Garbage Out

We have "history" with our parents. Over the years, hurt feelings and anger have built on both sides. Some of us find we're still stuck back in childhood patterns, often "getting back" at our old mother for feelings of deprivation and lack of love that go way back.

It's time to search our own motivation. Are we possibly just a teeny bit glad that irritating, domineering old Mom is now under our thumb? Are we still paying our taciturn father back for ignoring us when we were little?

There are an incredible number of seemingly adult people living lives dominated by old leftover emotions—psychological "garbage."

Their feelings about themselves are based on leftover feelings about their folks. "I can't please him anyway, so why try?" People who relate every failure and disappointment to their parents' treatment of them as children set themselves up for unhappiness.

What happened, happened. It's time to acknowledge it, to understand that Mom and Dad probably won't change, to forgive them for what they did to make us so miserable, and to carry on our own grown-up lives. We not only hurt our parents when we carry around anger, we also hurt ourselves. We let old garbage block us from going on.

More of Who We Were

Remember, we've been saying that human beings usually don't change personality styles as they age. They just become more of what they were. The nervous young girl who's never sure she looks pretty enough can become the elderly woman who piles on more and more makeup to look presentable to the outside world. The reserved young boy who prefers to be alone a great deal probably won't flower when he's old enough to go to the senior center. He may enjoy quiet, passive activities, but he's not likely to volunteer to plan a program.

People who are locked into roles need to act out their script. They need to follow the set of instructions a role provides right to the end of life. A young princess grows into a queen. A martyr needs to suffer and do a great deal of sighing. A care-giver needs to continue to take care of us, whether we need it or not. An ostrich needs to continue to deny and bury her head in the sand. If we keep this in mind, it makes it easier to deal with our elderly parents.

We Can't Force Them to Be Happy

The most dedicated do-it-yourselfers among us are convinced that if we find the right set of tools and materials we can rehab our parents. After all, we raised children to adulthood, didn't we?

But with parents we're not dealing with unformed personalities and we don't have the same kind of responsibility toward them.

It's not our role to plan their development and their future happiness. We only can take care of their physical needs, give them the help and support they need, and love them. *We can't force them to be happy.*

Because we care, we get "lovingly bossy" with them. We want them to enjoy their senior years. And if it's up to us, they'll enjoy them whether they want to or not! From the vantage point of our comparative youth, we're convinced that we have the answers to how they should handle their lives.

Freida Marcus, 90, suffers from a "geographic depression." In the winter she lives in Florida in a senior hotel with several ladies her age. They play cards and sit around the pool gossiping about their families. The hotel schedules many day trips and special events for its guests, so Freida lives a busy life.

Her son Hal, 60, is the family "rescuer." As soon as the hot season sets in, he flies down to Florida and moves his mother back up north to her apartment in Chicago. Freida lives in one of those high-rises on Lake Michigan that are populated with elderly widows. The trouble is, the ladies Freida knew there are now dead or living in a warm climate year-round. She'd like to stay in Florida all summer, but Hal and her doctor "won't let her." It's too hot.

Alone in her Chicago apartment, Freida gets depressed. She calls Hal and complains. "I'm alone every night. I don't know what to do with myself."

Then Hal falls into the solicitous rescuer role. "Why don't you go to the senior center and join in the activities there?"

"No. What would I do there?"

"Why don't you visit Aunt Cissy?"

"I can't stand my sister. She may be my sister, but I don't have to visit her. I'd rather be alone."

"Why don't we take a look at the North Shore Hotel? If you move there during the summers, you'll be with lots of ladies. They have bingo and luncheons, and there's good shopping nearby."

"I can't. And bingo is a waste of time."

And so it goes. Hal says, "Why don't you?" and Freida says, "I can't."

Freida has a real depression, but it's geographical. When she's in Florida, she takes care of her own social life and is so busy that Hal says, "When I call her, she can't wait to get off the phone. She's always on her way somewhere."

But in Chicago Freida *acts out her role in the script.* She sees her psychiatrist and takes her medicine, but to whatever suggestion is offered, she answers "I can't."

Freida "can't" help herself and improve her living situation because in Chicago she must act as though she needs rescuing. Her son devotes himself to rescue attempts, and unconsciously she plays the role of rescuee. If she stopped complaining and feeling blue, he wouldn't have to rescue her. Then when would she see him?

What should Hal do? He's been playing "why don't you" with his mother for years. It's not working. If she were busy doing what he suggests, she wouldn't have any reason to complain; so she's not going to follow his advice. He should accept the fact that he can't make his mother happy (at least not in Chicago) and stop his attempts to overcome what he calls her "stubbornness." He's doing all he can to help and support her. He must stop trying to rescue her.

If you're one of those people who has "big shoulders" and feels responsible for your parent's emotional needs, you're to be commended for your caring sensitivity. But watch out! If you insist on playing the rescuer, you're tempting Mama to take the rescuee role. Remember what happened when you jumped into fights between your children and rescued the whining one? He soon learned that he could get all your attention by whining.

This is an unconscious process. Neither you, the "savior," nor your parent intends for it to develop. But when you're working to save "poor old Mom," there can easily be a "poor old Mom" working just as hard to be helpless, sad, and eventually truly depressed.

Tyranny of the Weak

Just as in any relationship, our parent knows our strengths and weaknesses. "Ask Marilyn to do it," they say. "She's the responsible one."

When Mom starts turning over masses of responsibility to us, at first we're flattered. This proves we're adult at last! It feels good to be needed so much. "You're everything to me. What would I do without you?" she says.

Our ego swells the way it did the first time a needy boyfriend or girlfriend asked, "What would I do without you? I can't study. I can't sleep. You have to go out to dinner with me Saturday; I have to see you or I can't make it." Of course, we went. All that naked need laid at our feet was irresistible.

But when reality hit later, we discovered that we didn't like feeling responsible for another's happiness. We began to resent all those demands on our time. And then we felt guilty because we resented someone who needed us. And then we resented feeling guilty. Eventually, we "broke up." It wasn't fun having another person dominate us with the weapon of weakness.

We can't break up with our parents. *But we can refuse to accept the assignment.*

Mother says, "What would I do without you? I'd be lost. I couldn't live if you didn't take such good care of everything. My mind is at rest when you're in charge."

We respond, "Boy, are you in trouble if you're relying on me. My memory isn't so terrific anymore, and I make plenty of mistakes."

This message implies that we can't take over her entire life. We don't walk on water. The burden of living our own life plus hers would be impossible. We'll help her all we can, but she's not going to get away with handing over all the responsibility to us. She still must function because we both know she's capable of it.

In other words, we're refusing to respond to the misery signal Mom is beaming directly at us. If we call a moratorium on responding to "poor me" behavior, Mom will cast about for a new scenario. She loves and needs us, and she really doesn't want us to be steaming inside. So it's up to us to stop reinforcing excessive dependence.

How Much Venting Is Too Much?

In Chapter 3, "Sending Straight Signals," we talked about letting our parents "vent"—being there for them when they need to talk about their litany of problems, real or imagined. Usually, this unloading makes them feel appreciably better as long as we listen and take an active interest in their conversation.

What if the dumping gets out of hand? What if our conversations with our parents become nothing more than recitals of never-ending complaints? What if we keep edging toward the door with fantasies of hopping a plane for the Bahamas?

If we don't put a stop to it, we'll keep shortening our visits until ultimately we lean around the front door, say, "Hi, Mom," wave at her, and leave.

When your parent crosses that line between healthy venting and morbid obsession with sad tales and complaints, you can intervene. Here are some tips for coping with "over-venting."

Change the subject. Say, "We've spent enough time talking about unpleasant things. Let's talk about something else." Then find a topic that interests both of you, preferably something fresh. Perhaps you can talk about current events. Or if today's news is too disagreeable, ask your parent about something you've always wanted to know. There must be something about your parent or the family that has piqued your curiosity for years.

Every family has at least one hilarious family secret. Remind Dad about the time Uncle Arthur drove the wrong way down a one-way street and insisted all the other drivers were crazy. Or ask Mom to tell you again about how she feigned a headache and came home from a "blind date" at 8:30. Remembering funny incidents from the past will "get her mind off her troubles."

Tune out temporarily. If Mom is bent on a morning of moaning, excuse yourself and go to the kitchen for a glass of water. When you come back to the living room, try a new conversational tack. If she persists in reciting every pain, go for another glass of water. Eventually, she'll catch on and be willing to talk about other, more pleasant subjects.

Help your parent identify and define her problems. All therapists do this to get the patient to move from an emotional mode to an intellectual one. When you take the problem out of the feeling mode, you're helping your parent cope with her inner distress. Together, you're examining the anxieties in the cold light of day.

For instance, if Mom is a widow and can talk only about her sad existence, her loneliness, her bereavement, you can handle it by asking her questions. "What do you think you want to do now?" "What's your next step?" Your object is to make her think realistically about her situation—to disinvolve her from her emotional maelstrom. You can expect some resistance at first. After all, you've been a quiet, passive audience up to now. But if you're motivated by compassion, it will show in your tone, and Mom will gradually understand that you're trying to participate in her problem.

Help her to break her problems down into manageable pieces. When you divide her difficulties into categories—those problems you can address right now and those that cannot be changed—you will both be concentrating on how you can help.

Ian Smythe, 38, didn't expect to find himself the sole confidant and emotional prop for his peppy, attractive, 63-year-old mother, Elaine. His father had died of a heart attack on the golf course, leaving Elaine in an unexpected financial mess. The Smythes had lived an interesting, comfortable life. There was no reason to believe that after Harry died, Elaine would be a widow with money worries. But Ian's father had been a profligate spender. He'd left very little insurance, and the small savings were quickly snapped up by creditors.

Elaine was devastated. She'd not only lost her vibrant, happy-go-lucky husband but for the first time in her life, she was broke. She couldn't sleep at night. So she'd call Ian: "What shall I do? How shall I live? I've never worked a day in my life. I don't know how to do anything. I've never used a computer. What if I get sick? Where will I go? Should I sell the house?"

Ian was fast regretting that he lived in the same city as his mother. He wished he'd taken that transfer last year. What did a young, single guy know about those things? Why didn't his mother call her cousins?

Finally, Ian took his mother to a restaurant so they could plan her future. In her house, she tended simply to walk around wringing her hands. Here, in a public place, he was able to pin her down.

"Okay, Mother," Ian said, "we're going to look at your situation and start working just on one part of it. Okay?"

His mother nodded.

"Right. Now, I figure it this way. Your most pressing need is financial security. You'll have to sell the house. You won't get much because there's a second mortgage, but you ought to realize, oh, maybe thirty thousand dollars."

His mother gasped. "That's all?"

"Yes. But it's enough for a down payment on a little condo in Chestnut Hill."

"But Chestnut Hill is a very ordinary neighborhood!" Elaine protested.

"Yes, Mom, but it's safe. And it's what you can afford. It's also near a good bus line. If you don't learn to drive Dad's car, you'll need transportation. If you don't like the condo idea, you can sell the house and rent an apartment. But I really think you'd be better off owning something—tax breaks."

Elaine brushed away tears, but she said, "You're right, Ian. But how would I make the monthly payment? Your father..."

Ian said, "Mother, you're a very attractive woman. You have a lot of style and clothes sense. Have you ever thought about selling women's clothing at one of the nice specialty shops? You'd be great at it."

Elaine smiled, the first smile Ian had seen since Harry died. "Do you really think I could do that? I'm just a total loss at making change and wrapping things."

Ian reassured her. "You probably wouldn't have to make change or wrap anything. Just use your good clothes sense and nice manners and you'll be a top salesperson. I guarantee it!"

Elaine beamed. "Thank you, Ian. You've shown me a path out of this mess. Tomorrow morning I'm going to dress up and go job hunting. Maybe if I wear the right makeup I can pass for 55!"

Ian didn't promise his mother instant success or a wealthy future. But he did cut through her desperation and lead her into thinking about the next step. By showing her some alternatives to a bad situation, he helped her realize that she could take charge of the rest of her life.

When a parent is considering giving up his or her living situation and moving to a retirement facility, you can help her focus on the individual pieces of the puzzle. Talk it out with her. Is she thinking of moving because she's lonely? Maybe she can stay in her place and try to get involved in a volunteer or other group project. Is the rent too high for her? Perhaps you could look together for less expensive living arrangements. Is her health failing so that she can no longer care for the apartment? Talk to her about staying where she is but getting some help in the house. The more alternatives you can provide, the easier it is for her to make a decision.

Chipping away at what looks like an insurmountable mountain of problems gives both of you a better handle on Mom's situation. If your objective is to get Mom to think, not cry, you have to be careful not to confront her with hostility. Don't be judgmental or critical.

Remember, you're trying to help both of you so you can interact in a better way. Don't preface your comments with "Stop crying already!"

A Ray of Hope

As we fumble toward putting an end to conflicts with our parents and restructuring our relationship, we do have some strengths on our side:

1) We can take a hard look at Mom or Dad's provocative, unreasonable behavior and try to discover how it makes us feel.

2) We can admit that we're "feeding into" the system. We can admit that our responses are not working. We're getting angry, worked up, aggravated, guilty—we're playing out our role in the scenario in ineffective ways.

It's time to change our reactions so that we're no longer reinforcing and encouraging negative patterns. We can take a clue from the Quakers and use love, not war, in playing our part. And we can seek out methods that encourage our parents to compensate for their losses in healthy ways—by contributing to their community.

SEVEN

How to Help Our Parents Compensate Constructively

In Chapter 1 we discussed the many losses—sexual, occupational, and social—that beset our elderly parents. Much of their behavior, not to mention misbehavior, occurs because of those losses.

The grandmothers on Collins Avenue in Miami, dressed in tight jeans, high-heeled shoes, and wigs, seem to be trying to compensate for sexual losses. Senior citizens who depreciate the present—"Everything was better in the old days"—are really trying to compensate for their lost past. People try to compensate for loss of status in a variety of ways, from lording it over their children to picking fights with grocery clerks to becoming the neighborhood know-it-all.

One of the keys to building more successful relationships with our parents is to help them find *positive* ways of making up for their many losses. Successful compensators find ways of contributing to their families and to the world; they're flexible and strong enough to make lemonade from the lemons of growing old. By contributing their expertise and wisdom, they gain a sense of mattering. We all need to be needed, to the very last days of our lives.

Social institutions That Give People a Place

When the late Lillian Carter, mother of former president Jimmy Carter, joined the Peace Corps in her seventies, she was "giving back" to the world the benefits of her experience. Unfortunately, there aren't enough social institutions like the Peace Corps, where the energies of senior citizens can be channeled and used creatively. But gradually, as the need becomes painfully evident, answers are starting to come from grass-roots organizations and coalitions such as the Older Women's League and the American Association for Retired Persons.

These privately funded organizations are proving to be healthy stimuli for change. They've shown us that our parents can make things happen for themselves. In a world where you could ask the question, "Who speaks for seniors in America?" and get a lukewarm response, we're slowly seeing a turn-around. We're seeing grandparents taking college courses at greatly reduced tuition, retired men and women returning to the work force, older people getting a grip on their political "clout" and using it to lobby for legislation that protects their interests.

A recent study shows that the majority of American-born men report satisfaction with senior years. Sixty-two percent of them enjoy sharing household chores with their wives, and 45 percent are actively involved in baby-sitting their grandchildren. They have definite roles to fill and have added structure to their days. One 77-year-old admitted, "My son saw that I was getting depressed around the house, so he took me to an exercise class for men my age. Now I go to the 'Y' every day and take a two-mile walk with my wife every evening. I'm really enjoying my life."

Foreign-born men have a harder time. Often they had to leave school at an early age to keep their families going. Club work, bridge, golf—these were not part of their younger lives. So they entered retirement years with few inner resources to help fill the time. They don't understand why their children don't spend more time with them, and they are unwilling to learn new hobbies and meet new people.

There are many organized programs that provide a way for older people to contribute:

SCORE (Service Corps of Retired Executives). Sponsored by the U.S. Small Business Administration, SCORE is made up of retired business people and corporate executives who act as consultants to small businesses, arts organizations, and volunteer neighborhood groups. It's an excellent example of a social institution designed to use the talents of older people.

Foster Grandparents. In many cities, older people are registered and trained to give needed love and attention to latch-key children. Many foster grandparents are confined to their own homes, some in wheelchairs. But they maintain a telephone link with children who come home from school to an empty house. And those who are physically able to do so take lonely children on outings or just spend a day with them. This program has been successful in many towns and cities for several years because it provides a much needed opportunity for young children and seniors to feel useful. They both give the gift of their time and attention to each other.

"Acting Up." There's a group in Chicago called "Acting Up" that might serve as a prototype for similar groups elsewhere. It comprises retired people from a variety of backgrounds. They write and produce their own theater, which often is a presentation of oral history—telling the story of their pasts. Some of the people are retired professional actors. Others never stepped on a stage before. This innovative troupe "takes their show on the road" and performs at various community centers, hospitals, and nursing homes.

Hospital volunteers. In hospitals throughout the country older people are engaged in meaningful roles. At one metropolitan hospital a group of men acts as liaison with home-care patients. They call people to remind them of appointments and even pick them up and bring them into the hospital when necessary. Other hospitals use seniors to tend the information desk, deliver mail, and visit with patients. They fill in on many jobs that regular paid staff are too busy to handle. Of course, not all retired people enjoy the pleasant, if somewhat humdrum, aspects of jobs such as these. They need more responsible work, jobs they feel are worthy of their talents. Some retirees have to be as innovative as one former sales manager for a large company. He offered to look over the purchasing policy at a small-town Ohio hospital free of charge. In a matter of months, he found ways to improve the hospital's ordering policy and save the hospital thousands of dollars a year.

OWL (Older Women's League). This national organization of activists has more than one hundred groups across the country. If Mom is a believer in self-help organizations and likes to focus on social change, this is the organization for her. In their relatively short life (about twenty years), OWL has formed a caring, supportive sisterhood for midlife and older women. They lobby in their respective states for issues such as pay equity, insurance for dependent spouses, job training programs for displaced homemakers, adequate retirement benefits, and the like.

OWL functions on two levels for its members. They work to change legislation and, on an individual basis, they step in to help each other. There's a kind of neighbor-helping-neighbor mentality in the group that sets it apart from other national organizations. As one California member put it, "Sure, I'm concerned with national issues and changing times for all women, but when I'm in a crisis, I like to know that another OWL member will stand by me."

At the local level OWL is an important support resource. Dr. Margaret Huyck, president of OWL Illinois and professor in the Institute of Psychology at the Illinois Institute of Technology as well as a consultant to Metropolitan Family Services for the Chicago area, points up the issue of spousal impoverishment. "We are concerned with family care-giving issues and what happens when a woman's husband goes into a nursing home. Twenty years ago she might well have been depleted of all assets to pay for his care." Now, thanks to the advocacy and efforts of OWL and other organizations, we have national care-givers' legislation that protects the wife of a nursing home resident. She can keep their home, car, and personal possessions plus a modest amount of cash for her needs. The amount of money the spouse is allowed to keep in the bank varies with each state. Illinois is one of the states with a more generous allowance for the non-institutionalized spouse, around $16,000 a year.

If you'd like to know more about OWL, check your local telephone directory or write to their national headquarters:

> OWL National Office
> 666 Eleventh Street N.W.
> Suite #700
> Washington, DC 20001
> Phone: 202-783-6686
> Website: OWL_National.org

Senior Service Corps Programs

A group of outstanding service programs for seniors is now under the umbrella of Americorps, the Corporation for National Service, which sponsors a multitude of service programs for Americans who enjoy volunteering. The following programs are geared specifically for seniors. Many of the projects lend themselves to groups, like a golf league or bridge club or a church group. In this way friends can team up and volunteer together on a regular basis if they wish.

RSVP (Retired Senior Volunteer Program). This is one of the federal government's Older Americans Volunteer Programs. Each RSVP office is run according to the needs of the community. Your parent is provided with free transportation to and from the volunteer site, a real boon for many older people who no longer drive. Volunteers are given an orientation as well as inservice training and are assigned according to their skills. A fabulous cook, for example, would be matched to a low-income day care center where the main meal of the day is provided by the center. One former letter carrier says, "I had a talent for organization that I never realized. I always set up my route so that I finished earlier than the others. When I joined RSVP, they seemed to sense that in me, and now they have me setting up schedules at the local senior center. Before I came along, the social worker had to devote several hours of her week to organizing the weekly activities. She's been freed to concentrate on counseling, and I enjoy the challenge of making sure everything clips along."

The Senior Companion Program. Another federal program, SCP, is open to low-income people over the age of 60 and offers a unique way for people to contribute their skills in helping other senior people. Participants provide back-up to the homebound elderly, little services that enable the homebound to continue to live independently. Volunteers help with light shopping, accompany disabled people to the doctor's and dentist's offices, and act as listener and friend to those whose boundaries are four walls.

Senior companions get a small, tax-free stipend and transportation allowances. They're trained in how to locate appropriate community services for the homebound—an example of older people learning to make the system work for themselves and their peers. One senior companion, a retired domestic worker, says, "When I was a younger woman, I always volunteered at church. We visited the old ones who were stuck at home and needed someone to mail a letter for them or just sit and visit. The reason I like this program so much is that now I'm reaching out to people my age or a bit older who have nobody else to help. Even the churches are having trouble getting volunteers to do this kind of thing. Younger people are all so busy."

Foster Grandparents for Children with Special Needs. This federal program differs from other foster grandparent programs in that it's specifically geared to low-income older people who wish to work with handicapped children. Volunteers need persistence, kindness, and a loving heart. They receive 40 hours of pre-service orientation and monthly inservice training workshops. In return, they get similar benefits to the volunteers in the Senior Companion Program, hot meals on the job, accident insurance, and an annual physical examination. The non-tangibles include hugs, kisses, and the message that they are appreciated by their young friends. If you have a parent with a lot of love and warmth to give, he or she will be guaranteed a feeling of making a difference.

To learn more about these three federal government programs in your parents' locality, call 1-800-424-8867. It's toll free. Or check the Website—www.Americacorps.org. Just scroll through the Website and click on Seniorcorps.

Guides, docents, and receptionists at museums, zoos, and community art galleries are usually retired people. At the Monterrey Bay Aquarium in Monterrey, California, visitors are met at the door by a knowledgeable retired person wearing an identifying badge. He points out the lay of the land and shows tourists the high points of this unique, living museum. These volunteer guides are an invaluable asset and receive as much as they give. Says one elderly volunteer: "I meet people from all over the world. I can't wait to come here in the morning. My work here has opened a fascinating new world."

School Bells Ring – Are They Listening?

Maybe your Mom or Dad is one of those people who always told you, "When I get older, I'm going back to school. I want to learn all the things I never had time for before." But Dad is ensconced in his chair in front of the TV or following Mom around the house, checking to see if there's dust on the coffee table.

Now's the time to get him interested in one of the many adult education and college classes available at reduced cost to older people. Don't throw a batch of catalogs and course outlines down and announce, "Here. You always said you wanted to go back to school. Now do it!"

You may have to reassure Dad that he can still learn new material. Some older people do have a slower rate of learning new information. But what they might lack in memory skills, they can compensate for in accumulated wisdom. You can assure Dad that he will keep up with the class. His life-long habits of discipline and ability to concentrate on what's at hand will come to his aid.

One college professor says, "I prefer teaching older people. When I have a retired person in my class, I know we're going to have a stimulating discussion. Older people don't care about making an impression on classmates. When they have a question, they ask it. And they want answers. Some of the young people are busy trying to date the good-looking kid next to them or are worried about finding a job when they graduate. Older men and women concentrate on the course content. They keep me on my toes!"

You can help your parent come to a decision about what courses to take. Reading through a college catalog is like leafing through a French cookbook. We want to try it all. But you can pick out a few courses you think Dad will like and suggest he give them a try. You know your father's interests. Does he follow national politics? Then perhaps he'd enjoy a course in modern Russian politics. Has he always picked out tunes on the piano or liked popular songs of his era? Then maybe Dad would enjoy a course in the development of American jazz.

Many college campuses now set aside space and parking areas for a Retirement Learning Institute, an idea which has spread rapidly across the United States. The courses are not "busy work" or opportunities for retirees to get together and just chat. They are taught, by and large, by retired experts in their field. Often these experts are the same people who lead groups through the Grand Canyon or over the beaches of Costa Rica or to any other wonderful place where seniors travel.

Travel Ventures and Adventures

If you have traveled anywhere recently, you know that younger age groups are often outnumbered by seniors on the move. So popular has this idea become, especially with the growth of seniors with financial resources to indulge their travel desires, that there now exist travel companies like Grand Circle, Overseas Adventure Travel, Vantage, and others for people over 55 years of age. Chances are your parents know about this already. There seems to exist an extremely efficient network of travel specialists that simply find the senior market and then deluge them with brochures, letters, and the like. The advantages are many: trained and caring group leaders, itineraries usually set up so that travelers spend at least two nights in one place, congenial traveling companions. If your parent is in the doldrums, look into some of this literature, pick the destination you know your parent always wanted to see, and if you can spare the time, go with her or him. You'll be capturing quality time together, sharing an adventure, and providing your parent with a sense of security.

Your parent can combine the need to see what's just around the next bend with the need to know more about a variety of cultures and subjects with the *Elder Hostel* trips. These carefully crafted one-week seminars offer good companionship and professional seminar leaders, often retired college professors. The concept has become so popular that older travelers are now attending *Elder Hostel* programs throughout the world.

An added social dimension: often people traveling with senior travel groups or attending an *Elder Hostel* session make life-long friends among the participants. Frequently they will plan the next trip around the schedule of a friend they met on a previous trip. And it is not unheard of for wedding bells to ring for two people "of a certain age" who met and fell in love while stalking the giant turtles on a beach in Florida.

For more information on the multitude of programs *Elder Hostel* offers, contact them at:

Elder Hostel
11 Avenue de LaFayette

Boston, MA 02111
Call: 617-426-7788
Visit their Website at: www.Elderhostel.org

Do Your Homework

Once you've identified your parent's possible areas of interest, you
can do the leg work and investigate what's available locally. To learn
what's happening in your parent's community, check the local newspaper, library notice board, and YMCA, church, and synagogue bulle-
tins. You should also contact your state or local office or department
of senior citizen services.

It's important to function merely as a resource or back-up person
when you're helping to find worthwhile ways for your parents to contribute their gifts and energies. If you push too hard, your parents may
view your efforts as interference. You might casually mention some
program or event you think will interest Mom or Dad: "Mom, did you
read in the paper about the new quilting club? It's really interesting
because it's inter-generational. They have members from age 92 down
to 15. They meet right at the Presbyterian Church on Laurel Avenue."
You've planted the seed; now it's up to Mom to start thinking about it.
In a few weeks, you can bring it up again: "I saw a quilting club display
at the Women's Club. Some of their things aren't nearly as good as
yours. Did you happen to notice it in the display case?"

Many older people resolutely refuse to go to a senior center no
matter how great you think it is. They respond much better to activities that are not labeled "senior," and they really don't want to be in
groups made up solely of older people. The more you suggest going
down to the senior center for bingo, the more they resist. If your parents have those attitudes, look for activities that take in a mix of ages.

Is It Okay to Find Mom a Job?

Many people don't feel worthwhile unless they're paid for their
work. If you think your parent feels that way, sit down with him or
her and brainstorm. What are her skills? What does she love doing?

Does she enjoy working alone in her own living room? Would she rather go out and work with a group?

If you think about it, the possibilities are there. It's a question of identifying her interests and then letting others know about her "employability." One New Orleans woman who's a skilled calligrapher found herself more embroiled in doing wedding invitations for her daughter's friends than she'd bargained for. Another has used her baking skills to start a little business. She says, "One day I offered a homemade doughnut to the young man who delivered my groceries. Next thing I knew, his mother called and ordered three dozen doughnuts for her office. Then her neighbor called and asked if I could make cinnamon sweetrolls for *her* office, and I've been busy ever since."

Many people in our parents' generation developed skills as children that have almost died out—tatting, quilting. applique work, hand-tied fishing lures, stuffed animals made from men's work socks, dolls fashioned from wooden clothes pegs. With the nostalgia craze plus the resurgence of appreciation for hand-made items, such skills are being revived.

One 82-year-old from Elkhorn, Wisconsin, can't keep up with the demand for his carved wooden duck decoys. He says, "My son took some of my carvings to a little art fair in Milwaukee three years ago, along with a stack of cards with my name and address. I started getting calls from all over the Midwest. At first, it was too much for me to handle. Now I have found a neighbor boy who likes to whittle, and he's my assistant. Sometimes I long for the good old days when I did a lot more relaxing on long winter nights. But I have to tell you, I feel younger now!"

In many states older people with precious handicraft skills can put their talents to good use through an innovative organization called "Elder Crafters Helping Others." Handy seniors meet at senior centers on a regular basis and produce specific handcrafted items that are donated to charities. Crafters make items like children's slippers, cosmetic bags, baby quilts, and the like. The finished items are distributed to hospitals, homeless shelters, and community health clinics. Janet Langlois, executive director of this unique organization, says, "Our whole mission is to keep seniors creative and productive. The more you use your mind, the better it works." To find out how your parent can get involved in this network, contact:

Elder Craftsmen, Inc.
610 Lexington Avenue
New York, NY 10022
Phone: 212-319-8128
Fax: 212-319-8141
E-mail: eldercraftsmen@mindspring.com
Website: www.eldercraftsmen.org

Now Mom or Dad Can Swap Goods for Services

One elderly lady who still maintains her own bungalow can't afford to pay expensive plumbing and handyman bills. She says, "My kids put up an ad at the senior center, offering to swap my home-baked bread and rolls in exchange for home repair projects. We located a gentleman who now does all the little fix-it jobs around the house for two loaves of bread and a dozen sweetrolls per week. Last week his grandson came over and offered to take down the storm windows if I'd provide homemade cupcakes for his sister's birthday party."

Senior women are always in demand as baby-sitters. If Mom is lonely for the patter of little feet and nobody in the family is filling that need, you might work up a leaflet and distribute it in the neighborhood. Mom can either accept money or ask for services such as electrical repairs, shoveling snow, or carrying heavy grocery bags.

It takes some creativity and ingenuity on our part as well as our parent's to work out the right formula. Again, our function should be that of a resource person, the back-up and second-stringer. It's their show. But we can lay the groundwork, do the research and running around, present them with a few possible scenarios, show them ways they can find a satisfying volunteer job, or help them develop a little business or barter system for services.

On the theory that two heads are better than one, we can suggest practical ways for them to use the skills and interests they've always taken for granted. We can be the catalyst that keeps them connected to the world. The important thing is to work together.

Taking Care of Yourself As Well As Your Parent

Some of us are ready for the caretaker role. Among unmarried women and a smaller number of men who always lived at home, caring for one's parent is a natural outgrowth of the aging process. As Mama gets older and can no longer be as physically active as before, the child gradually takes on caretaker responsibilities. In other families, in which all of the children have left home, there's often one sibling, married or single, who simply steps in and assumes responsibility.

In a study conducted by Dr. Ursula Lehr for the Institut für Gerontologie at the University of Heidelberg, "Elderly Daughters Caring for Their Old Parents," researchers studied 100 daughters of middle-class German families. These women ranged in age from 55 to 70 and were caring for parents or parents-in-law between 78 and 98 years old. Nearly 60 percent were married; the rest were single.

This study and many others conducted by the Institut in the past ten years bear out that "family-care is daughter-care" and that "Very often the aging daughter has to take over the care of parents at an age at which she would have her last chance of reentering the labor force or taking over extra-familial roles in social organizations, political organizations, church, community, etc. These extra-familial roles would extend her own life-space and offer her the stimulation necessary for her mental development and psycho-physical well-being in old age."

The daughters fell into two distinct groups: those who were coping well and those who were experiencing conflict and stress.

The copers (roughly half of the women studied) "were able to fulfill their own needs, to develop their own interests, and were ready to assert their interests to their parents."They had put the parent into perspective—as an important variable in their lives but not the most important.They also felt free to ask other family members, friends, and neighbors to spell them so they could get out of the house and pursue their own paths.

The other 50 percent of the women in the study were exhausted and defeated by trying to cope single-handedly. They reported feeling stressed by the restriction of their freedom and lack of time to take vacations or pursue a hobby.

Researchers also discovered that coping families were those in which the aging parent added her efforts to running the household. When the daughter encouraged the mother to take responsibility and fulfill some functions, the relationship was smoother. Trouble reared its head when the daughter "took over" and treated the mother as another child in the home. We've already discussed how shut off and useless the older person without a role tends to feel. When a caretaking child includes Mom or Dad in family life, no matter how limited in capacity, he or she still has a place. A parent confined to a wheelchair can still help make a salad for dinner, handle the family sewing, or fix a lamp cord.

The Sacrificial Daughter—It's a Lonely Job

In one extended farm family, the younger daughter moved back home after an early widowhood. Although there are nine brothers and sisters, she virtually handles the care of her aged father single-handedly. She accepts this role because she truly is a gifted caretaker. She cheerfully says, "I was a frustrated nurse, I think. I loved feeling useful, and when my kids grew up, I was always finding someone in the church who needed help. I'm doing an important job taking care of Pa, and I know he needs me. But I'm always tired!"

These unsung, under-appreciated caretakers are often burdened unfairly. Frequently, there's a "let my sister do it" attitude among the siblings. And the caretaker feeds into that by not asking for assistance. *The burden of caring for an aging relative needs to be shared*

How to Get Help from Your Siblings

1) Involve everyone in the family. Of course, they're all busy and can only spare Mother an hour's visit on Sunday. And, of course, they feel you're doing such a great job that they wouldn't "dare interfere" with the way you're running the show. These are both excellent dodges to keep you tied to the job while they deny the reality of the situation. You must express your exhaustion and need to get away. You can always remind them, "If I get sick, I'll have to send Mother to your house."

Demand some time for yourself, and keep after them until you work out an arrangement. Even the busiest executive can spare one evening a week to sit with his parent. Try to keep in mind the following:

You're not asking for something unreasonable. It's only right and fair that each of the siblings takes some responsibility in a parent's care.

You're not the only one in the family who can do the job. Don't be taken in by remarks such as, "Rosemary is the only one of us who can handle Mother. She's just a wonder. I can't handle it myself. I just fall apart." This is one of the oldest family tricks known to excuse laying the burden on the "sacrificer" of the family. Of course your brothers and sisters care about you, but if you don't make noises about needing help, they'll let you carry on alone.

2) Sit down with your siblings and work out the financial arrangements if you have not already done so. If your mother or father cannot be left alone, then ask family members to contribute to the cost of a practical nurse or sitter for those times when you need to go out. After all, if you weren't the "resident care-giver," they'd have to pay a great deal more than the cost of an occasional substitute.

3) If you intend to be the primary care-giver for the rest of your parent's life, you'll need your physical and emotional strength. The only way you can continue without feeling beaten down is by taking

care of yourself You're entitled to your own physical and emotional health—you deserve it!

As soon as you get additional help, continue with the activities you've always enjoyed. Or develop new hobbies or take a part-time job that brings you satisfaction and the opportunity of being with other people.

To cope effectively, you must be realistic. Accept the fact that you can't handle this alone, no matter how much love and understanding you have to give. You need help, and you need to feel free to ask for it. There is no reason to feel guilty. You can be a better daughter or son when you realize your own limits.

Getting Help When You're Caring for a Parent Who's Confused

In a recent study conducted by the Department of Psychiatry and Behavioral Sciences at the Johns Hopkins University School of Medicine, 55 care-givers of patients with dementia talked about their feelings. The majority (48 out of 55) said they felt sad, angry, frustrated, depressed, and tired most of the time. And over half of the respondents had given up their friends, jobs, or meaningful volunteer work.

Caring for a parent with reduced cognitive ability is hard; it takes its toll on the family. Typically, the burden falls to one member of the family—often a daughter. Other family members may criticize her efforts, but generally they offer minimal support. "You handle it" is the phrase most often heard by these brave souls. As one unmarried daughter of an 80-year-old mother with Alzheimer's puts it, "I love my mother and I want to help her, but I wish my brothers and sisters would pitch in. They don't seem to realize that I'd like to go to a play or out to dinner with friends once in a while."

In the Johns Hopkins study and others like it, the key factor in successfully dealing with the cognitively impaired parent is social support. Fortunately, with the "graying of America" we're beginning to look at this type of care-giving and the enormous strains it puts on families. There are social agencies and hospital programs that provide relief. In some communities there are day care centers where you can bring your parent for a full day of activities and training in reality orientation by a professional staff of social workers, recreation workers, and psychologists.

Others offer sitter services in your home. You can find information on these and many other programs if you do some digging. Start with your doctor, your local hospital, your local social service agency, and your state mental health association. For information on this and other issues of coping as a care-giver, a grass roots organization called Children of Aging Parents (CAPS) can be an invaluable aid. CAPS began as a local support service and has mushroomed into a national resource for care-givers. To learn more contact them at:

> Children of Aging Parents
> 1609 Woodbourne Road
> Suite 302A
> Levittown, PA 19057
> Phone: 215-945-6900
> Fax: 215-945-8720
> Toll free: 1-800-227-7294

For an overview and approximate costs of both help in the home and at day care centers, contact:

> American Association of Retired Persons
> 1909 K Street N.W.
> Washington, DC 20049
> Phone: 202-434-2277

> The National Council on Aging
> 409 Third Street S.W.
> Suite 200
> Washington, DC 20024
> Phone: 202-479-1200
> Fax: 202-479-073 5
> Website: www.ncoa.org

Why Ostriches Get Headaches, Too

While it's demanding and stressful to be a live-in or live-nearby care-giver, adult children who live some distance away learn sooner or later that they can run but they can't hide from the problem.

Geraldine lives over 1,000 miles away from her mother. Up until now she has managed to avoid thinking about Mom's problems. Two years ago when her mother's debilitating arthritis made it impossible for her to carry on alone, Mom moved in with Gerry's sister in their home town of Helena, Montana.

A "wunderkind," Gerry sailed through college, married, went to graduate school, had two children, divorced, got her Ph.D., and married again. At the age of 47, she's riding high—in line for a full professorship in the English department of her respected, small college in California. Her friends all say, "Gerry's on a fast track."

Gerry is one of those women with energy to burn. She runs four miles a day before classes and looks ten years younger than her actual age.

But recently she has not been feeling her usual glowing self. Her sister has been calling from the family home in Helena with distressing messages: "Gerry, I need some help with Mom. Can you come some weekend so we can talk about it? I have a bad back, and I just can't manage getting Mom in and out of the wheelchair. We have to consider our next step."

Gerry is annoyed and upset by her sister's calls. Her mother has taken to calling, too, sometimes talking in a frightening rambling way. Gerry feels put-upon much of the time now. "What do they want from me?" she asks her husband. "I send them money every month as it is. My sister should find a good nursing home if she can't handle it."

Gerry goes to her doctor one day, complaining of headaches and problems with sleeping. After carefully investigating and ruling out other causes, her doctor astounds her by telling her that she's suffering from what he refers to as "stress syndrome." She, who runs four miles a day, handles a demanding, competitive career and a family, and looks great! Impossible!

Even at long distance, Gerry's emotional responses to her mother's situation are taking their toll. She's been "hiding out" in California, effectively erecting a smokescreen of busyness to avoid thinking about her mother, but her body has been reacting to what's really going on—Gerry's concern and guilt. The most dedicated ostrich eventually gets caught. The plain facts of our parent's aging and the way we respond have a way of sneaking up on us.

Managing Your Stress

When you're caring for an aging parent, you're likely to feel fatigued and depressed. You spend an afternoon with your frail and ailing father and come home drained. Yet the other parts of your life—your career, household, relationships with family members and friends—still need your time and energy. The demands pile up, and if you haven't learned to control the situation, your body gives you warning signals.

Racing pulse, headaches, stomach pains—these are sometimes bodily reactions to psychological pressures. And because we live in the modern world, we use the catch-all phrase "stress" to explain our physical reactions.

What is stress? Dr. Hans Selye, who published his findings several years ago, is still considered a world authority on stress. He determined that vital functions such as blood flow and hormonal activity are influenced by mental perceptions. We may not have to face the tiger at the entrance to our cave as our primitive ancestors did, but we have the same "fight or flight" response to demanding situations. When animals (including us!) perceive a situation as life-threatening, their bodies get ready to do battle or run. Our muscles tense. Our pulse races. We breathe rapidly and shallowly. We sweat. We feel a cold, hard rock in the pit of our stomach. Our hands and feet feel icy because the blood has rushed to our brain. With no tigers to confront or escape, modern human beings react instead to our twenty-first-century high-stress equivalents: divorce, loss of a loved one, job changes—and the pain, loss, bewilderment, anxiety, and guilt we feel about an aging parent.

Dr. Selye described our physical responses as "General Adaptation Syndrome." Over the years, our body adapts to the "tiger at the door." The stress hormones gather themselves for action even when there is no need to fight or fly. Eventually, these mobilized hormones cause wear and tear on our bodies and lower our resistance to injury, infection, and disease. The result may be ulcers, high blood pressure, heart disease, colitis, headaches, frequent colds, and other infections.

Caring for an aging parent is a stressful job. You have all the pressures and uncertainty of a fast-paced advertising office where the client must be satisfied. Account executives and copywriters never know where the next zinger is coming from. New crises is the name of the game. In many ways, care-givers for elderly parents suffer the same stresses.

But there are some specific things you can do that will help your body deal with stress:

1) *Eat properly.* Make sure you get plenty of fruits, vegetables, high-fiber cereals and grains, and two glasses of low-fat milk or the equivalent every day. Cut down on fats, fried foods, and processed foods that are loaded with sodium. Your daily intake should be made up of lean meat, fish, or chicken/turkey *without* skin or fat.

Make sure you drink six to eight glasses of water a day. The combination of water and high-fiber cereal foods helps to move waste from your body quickly and efficiently. You feel lighter and more energetic when your digestive system is functioning smoothly.

2) *Enjoy your food.* Take time. If you're in the habit of bolting breakfast while reading the morning newspaper, you may want to change. Pictures and stories of war, famine, random shootings, and the other joyous news faithfully reported by our morning newspapers, do not go down well with food. Of course, you want to be informed, but try not to ingest your news with your cereal.

3) *If you're not exercising on a regular basis, now is the time to begin.* Your goal should be to select an exercise that you genuinely like, one that makes you feel good, and one that benefits your body and mind.

You hear a lot about *aerobic exercise.* If you're not involved with fitness, you may think all aerobic exercise is strenuous pushing, straining, and gasping. Not so. Aerobic exercise is beneficial because it carries oxygen to all your muscles, especially the heart. It's continuous activity, as opposed to spurt-like bursts of exertion (e.g., shoveling snow) that can be harmful.

Brisk walking, running, swimming, bicycling—these are all helpful aerobic exercises. To be effective, aerobic exercise must be practiced for a minimum of twenty minutes three times a week. So if you live a hectic life, you can still fit in this minimum of exercise.

Start out slowly. Let's assume you've decided that brisk walking fits your schedule and sounds like something you can handle (given the shape you're in right now). Buy a good pair of athletic shoes, pick your walking site, and get started. Walk briskly, swing your arms, and breathe regularly. If you're exhausted after ten minutes, stop. On your next try, you can push it to eleven minutes. Later, to twelve. And so on.

After exercising, let your body cool down. Slow your brisk walk to a gentle stroll. When you reach your door, stretch your legs, arms, and torso. Take a shower if it's possible.

One 55-year-old woman who's responsible for the care of her 91-year-old mother says, "I've come to look forward to my swimming times as fun. At first I gasped like a beached whale after ten laps. Little by little, I increased my endurance. When I swim I don't worry about anything. There's something soothing about the regimen—side stroke for ten, back stroke for ten, crawl for ten, then start over. I don't have to plan anything. I don't have to think about what I'm doing. I just get into my program and stay with it for a half-hour. It's the most mindless, relaxing thing I do."

4) *Take daily time for yourself.* In addition to the time you spend exercising, make sure you take a few minutes a day to listen to music, call a friend, enjoy a new food, read a magazine—whatever makes you feel pampered. If you're a dedicated clothes horse, treat yourself to the latest copy of *Vogue* or *Gentleman's Quarterly.* If you've always wanted to learn how to make chocolate mousse, find a recipe, buy the ingredients, and set aside time to try it.

5) *Buy yourself a little present occasionally.* This can range from giving yourself a cup of cappuccino in a new cafe to buying a cassette of a favorite song. It needn't be expensive, just something that lifts your spirits. Buying fresh flowers for your office desk or your home qualifies as a present.

6) *Try to laugh every day.* Deep belly guffaws are not only good for the soul—they relax tensed abdomen and chest muscles. Laughing makes you feel "up," at one with the universe. And when you feel up and look happy, you'll effect others with your positive outlook. You need the support of your friends and co-workers now, if only to remind you there's an interesting world out there that you're still part of.

7) *Check your community for a yoga or stress-reduction class.* The gentle stretching movements of yoga induce a healthy mental balance. No matter how tied in knots we may be, a yoga class with a trained instructor can work wonders on our stressed body. Stress-reduction classes have the same magical effect. While we practice

deep breathing and visualization of pleasant surroundings we can go to in our mind, we are setting up healthy patterns of response. For further information on yoga concepts and programs, contact:

The American Yoga Association
513 S. Orange Avenue
Sarasota, FL 34236
Phone: 1-800-226-5859

How Not to Handle Stress

1) *Don't use alcohol as a crutch.* Recent studies have shown that the moderate use of alcohol can actually be beneficial. An occasional drink before dinner can have a calming effect on frazzled nerves. According to the *New England Journal of Medicine,* a moderate amount of alcohol increases the amount of high-density lipoproteins in our bloodstream. And these lipoproteins decrease the negative effects of cholesterol. So, if you're having a scotch-and-water two or three times a week as a way of relaxing with friends or family, you're not on the road to alcoholism.

But if you're drinking alone and drinking as a response to feelings of resentment and misery, you're in the danger zone. Be especially alert if you come from a family of heavy drinkers. There is strong evidence that some families have a genetic intolerance for alcohol. Some people should never drink at all. Their bodies don't metabolize liquor, wine, and beer properly, and they become drunk quickly, losing control of themselves and often blacking out. If you find yourself taking refuge in liquor to handle your stress, start immediately to change your pattern. Excessive drinking is no solution and can only damage your life as well as your ability to cope with your aging parent.

2) *Excessive smoking is a common and extremely unhealthy response to stress.* One beleaguered son whose disabled father lives in a nursing home and periodically threatens to jump out the window, admits, "I gave up smoking two years ago. When Dad started acting up, I went straight from his room to the nearest drugstore and bought a carton of my old brand. Now I'm back to two packs a day. Am I worried? Yes. Can I quit? I'm trying."

Smoking is physically addictive, and when we quit, we feel bad for a while—nervous, irritable, dizzy, depressed, tired, even constipated. Some doctors feel that this discomfort can be alleviated by a carefully planned gradual withdrawal. Peter Miller, Ph.D., founder and former director of the Hilton Head Health Institute in Hilton Head, South Carolina, offers clues to quitting:

Assessment. Write down when you smoke (after lunch, coffee break, etc.); where you smoke (at your desk at work, in your car, etc.); and when you smoke more than usual (at a party, in a new situation, etc.).

Motivation. Identify how important it is for you to quit. Are you concerned about your health? Are your friends nagging you to quit? Is it more important for you to take control of your life than it is to smoke? This is vital. If your desire to take control is strong enough, you will find it easier to quit.

Commitment. Announce to your friends and family that you're going to quit. Saying it aloud validates your commitment, and you're more likely to follow through on a promise you've made to others.

Withdrawal. Have a deadline date in mind right from the beginning. Then start decreasing your cigarette intake over a period of three to five days. You may find changing brands to a low-nicotine variety helpful during this withdrawal period.

In order for you to stay off cigarettes, it sometimes helps to find a good substitute. Some people swear by sugar-free gum or low-calorie candies. It's an excellent idea to take up a new activity such as meditation or exercise, something that serves to relax you the way you thought smoking did. Also, break the chain of associations. If you always smoked when you called your best friend, then have a cup of tea while you talk on the phone. Or keep a glass of water nearby.

3) *Taking solace in food is another common response to stress.* There are two kinds of people: those who lose their appetite in times of stress and those who have been known to break into cupboards to find the chocolate sandwich-cookies. If you find yourself grabbing whatever is available and gobbling, you're part of the second group. Good food is a nice bonus life gives us. But when we eat

out of nervousness or sadness, food ceases to be a pleasure and becomes a stop-gap cure for anxiety.

If your clothes are getting tight and you observe an extra chin that seems to have taken up residence under the chin you're familiar with, it's time to take stock of things. Ask your doctor if he can recommend a diet center. You'll not only get back on the path of eating nutritionally sound meals but you'll also find a lot of group support. Weight loss groups are made up of people who've had to struggle with overeating at some point. They know how extra pounds can batter your self-esteem. They're a much better alternative than those so-called quick-loss diets that starve you of important vitamins and minerals. If you take the weight off slowly, in the meantime learning good, new eating habits, you'll be able to maintain the weight you want.

4) *Stay away from too much coffee, cola, chocolate, and non-herbal tea.* Stimulants may pep you up, but they'll also can make your heart race and your hands tremble. Why add caffeine to your problems? Caffeine products can be fine in moderation, and if you dearly love that morning cup of mocha java, don't deny yourself. But try to confine your coffee intake to two cups a day.

The key to handling stress is to feel in control. In your relationship with your parent, chances are that guilt and hidden fears are contributing to your feelings of defeat and helplessness. When you confront those guilty, fearful feelings, you're taking the first step toward controlling them, putting them in their place so you can be free to enjoy life.

The Anatomy of Guilt: What's It All About?

Guilt is learned behavior. The infant who tears the bunny wallpaper off his bedroom wall feels no guilt. He's just doing what comes naturally—in this case, exploring the world around him. As yet, he has no sense of right and wrong. He's just doing what infants do.

We learn guilt as we grow up. The first time we feel, "Oh, I did something bad," we're catching on to what guilt is about. Our feelings of guilt are feelings of self-disapproval. The teacher in our minds shakes an admonishing finger at us. We feel a sense of failure, a conviction that "we're not good enough," the nagging certainty that we didn't measure up, that one way or another we blew our part in a relationship.

Feeling guilty lowers our self-esteem. But we don't like feeling uncomfortable and wrong about ourselves. Because we're human, we seek ways to increase our self-esteem. So we try to compensate for our guilty consciences.

How do we compensate? In two ways:

1) *We repent.* We feel sorry about flying off the handle or dropping a caustic comment or avoiding another person.

2) *We atone.* We try to make up for our bad actions. If we feel guilty about the way we snapped at Mom over the phone last week, on our next visit we bring her a raspberry tart from the French bakery or invite her to the movies.

What Methods Do We Use to Avoid Guilt?

Life is nicer when we don't feel guilty. So we find ways to help ourselves avoid the unpleasant nibble of guilt:

1) *We try to placate.* When Mom is crying about being old and infirm or being alone, we put on what we hope is a reassuring smile and say, "Don't feel so bad." Placating her is our attempt to help her feel better. And when Mom feels better, we can feel better about ourselves.

2) *We justify ourselves.* We explain and apologize. We try to rationalize. If we haven't visited Mom in a few weeks, we tell her, "I'd be over to see you on Saturday but I have to bring the car in, and then I have to finish up some overtime, and besides, I think I'm coming down with a cold." We're not fooling anyone with these elaborate explanations, but it's one of the ways we try to avoid guilt.

3) *We get angry.* Self-righteous anger impels us as we leave our parent's apartment and mumble to ourselves in the elevator: "I'm so nice to him and look how he yells at me." It's more comfortable for us to feel angry than to be consumed with guilt.

Let Me Off At the Next Stop

With aging parents, most of us end up feeling guilty at some point. We feel how unhappy they are, how limited in their social scope, how difficult for them to deal with poor health. We let them "get away" with a lot of inappropriate behavior because of our guilty feelings. And the more we let them manipulate us, the angrier we get, and that gives us even *more* guilt.

How do we get off the guilt train?

We can start by looking at the stimulus. What behavior on our parent's part is setting off our guilt response? Instead of wandering around in a miasma of generalized, debilitating guilt, try to locate the source. What is Mom doing or saying to make me feel so terrible?

Now look at your own behavior. Ask yourself "What am I doing wrong?" or "What am I not doing right?" Sometimes it's helpful to write it down. Try to analyze your actions (or inactions). Are you unconsciously trying to take over Mom's life and telling her how to live it? Are you treading on her feelings by refusing to talk about real issues? Are you staying away because she gets on your nerves? Or are you pretending Dad has enough money to live on, even though you suspect that he's just scraping by?

Stop telling yourself, "I'm doing all I can." If that were true, you wouldn't feel so guilty.

You probably are trying your hardest to do the right things for your folks. But if what you're doing isn't working—stop doing it. You're only perpetuating a bad pattern.

Take your share of blame if a bad relationship with your parents has developed. Admit that your halo has slipped. You are, indeed, human, and all your good intentions have not brought success. But it's not too late. You can change.

It's Your Choice

Though we often feel helplessly guilty, we're not. *We have a choice.* We can decide whether it's better to resent doing what our elderly parent wants 100 percent of the time or to say "no" and feel guilty.

Guilt feelings actually allow us to do what we want to do. They're the price we pay for getting off the hook. Guilt is what enables us to go out of town.

Although you don't see Mom as much as she would like, your guilt actually expresses your good intentions. You have a choice: spend your vacation with your mother or leave town and feel a little bad about it. Perhaps you really would like to spend some of your vacation time with Mom, taking her shopping and the like, but those two weeks are the only time you have away from a stressful job. So you *choose* to go out of town. By feeling guilty, you permit yourself to claim good intentions: "I'd like to spend more time with Mom, but I just can't do everything."

You have to decide how much guilt you can tolerate as well as analyze how big a role guilt is playing in your life. Can you live with your current level of guilt? Or is it literally making you sick or souring your relationships with loved ones?

Ernie Bachman, 58, was raised to be a "man's man." The son of an army officer, Ernie spent a lot of time with his father during his childhood and adolescence. They went trapshooting and fishing together and enjoyed a companionable low-key relationship. His father kept his emotions under wraps and Ernie did, too.

Ernie got along well with his mother, but he kept a respectable male distance. When it came to problems, he handed them over to his wife, Frances.

Now Ernie's mother is growing frail and increasingly dependent. A victim of osteoporosis, she has had several hospitalizations. Whenever Ernie goes to visit her, he makes sure Frances is with him. "My wife knows how to handle Mom better than I do," Ernie claims. "I don't have the patience. I can't stand Mom's complaining and crying."

By turning the bulk of the day-to-day responsibility for his mother over to his wife, who fortunately accepts the duty as her lot in life, Ernie is able to maintain a tolerable relationship with his mother.

"I feel very guilty at times," Ernie admits. "I take care of all Mom's financial needs, but I just can't be with her too much. I feel guilty about laying it all on Frances. But, if it's a choice between seeing less of my mother and feeling guilty or seeing Mom as much as she would like and watching my hands shake for half an hour afterward, I'll take the guilt."

Ernie's position is reasonable and adult, as long as it doesn't drive Frances to the brink of divorce. He's not copping out of his responsibility to his mother—after all, he's paying her bills. But he's aware of his own emotional needs and limitations. He isn't able to satisfy all of his mother's expectations. And he's fortunate enough to have a wife who's willing to pick up the slack. Guilt is the price that Ernie has to pay for his adjustment. He can afford it—as long as it doesn't take too great a toll on his relationship with his wife. Ernie has *chosen* to accept a certain amount of guilt. His guilt lets him think of himself as a "good guy" rather than an ungrateful child.

How Do We Accept Our Parent's Vulnerability?

We see our parents growing frail and forgetful, and our tendency is to rush in and try to fix their lives. We want to protect them from the tigers lurking in the night of their old age. We feel guilty and fearful because we can't save them from inexorable aging and, eventually, death.

Like overprotective parents, we don't know how to let go. We hang on tightly because we're afraid for their safety. For the old, it often is a jungle out there. Every day we hear accounts of elderly people being mugged and thrown to the sidewalk. But we must keep in mind that *we can't protect them from everyday living* any more than we can follow our kids to school to be sure no harm befalls them. We have to accept that we're not divine or all-seeing. Our 78-year-old mother has been taking care of herself for a long time. We have to *trust* her now, trust the instincts that brought her this far. Otherwise, we'll be living in a state of constant anxiety that will ruin our lives and drive our poor parent to distraction.

John Gilbert's mother, Pauline, lives in a high-rise near a city park. Each day during the nice weather, she takes her cane and heads for "her bench" in the park. At the age of 83, she is confined to the square block near her building because she has great difficulty in walking; the park constitutes her social life.

And that social life is what worries John! One day he went to see Pauline during his lunch hour and was appalled to find his elegant mother sitting on "her bench" with some of the retired men who lived in rented rooms nearby.

He couldn't wait to tell his wife that evening. "We have to do something. They'll follow her home and hit her on the head. For all I know she's giving them money. You know what a soft touch she is."

John's wife, Rosemary, disagreed. "Look, your mother is a sensible woman. Years ago, she showed me how to pin money in my bra. She never carries more than a few dollars with her. She's told me that. She's aware of the transient nature of the neighborhood."

But John became obsessed with moving his mother into the safe suburbs. "Anything can happen to her there. She can get hit by a car or a bus when she crosses the boulevard. One of those old guys could carry a knife. You just never know."

For months John alternately begged and bullied his mother to move out of the apartment to a better area.

Finally, Pauline shouted at him. "What are you so afraid of? I have to die sometime. If I worried about a bus hitting me or somebody attacking me, I'd just have to give up living. And I'm not ready to do that! Now leave me alone!"

Rosemary finally settled the argument. She said to her mother-in-law: "You know how we have to be cautious of strangers. John's so worried about you. Why don't we figure out a way to put his mind at rest? I've been talking to the director at the nursing school in the neighborhood. A few of the student nurses get off at 3:00 and could be at your place by 3:15. They'd walk you over to the park and just catch up on their homework while you chat with your friends. They wouldn't interfere, I promise you. But John wouldn't worry so much about a bus hitting you. I'd really appreciate it, Mom, because he's driving me crazy with his anxieties."

In this way, Rosemary was able to "put the blame" on John without ever suggesting that the park companions might be objectionable. She let her mother-in-law keep her dignity and still maintain some control over the situation. Rosemary was insightful enough to see that Pauline needed to plan her own social life, inappropriate as it may seem to her son.

Anna Mostak tells a similar story. Her younger, unmarried son David, a 51-year-old stockbroker, panics when she's not well.

He calls her two or three times a day. "What's wrong, Ma? You sound so tired."

"So you'll sound tired when you're 84. Wait and see."

Anna survived World War II in Eastern Europe. She says, "I've lived a good life in this country. I don't expect to be young again. I wish he'd understand that."

David drags Anna from doctor to doctor trying to make her perfect. She has a bad heart, diabetes, and failing eyesight. Anna is getting the finest medical care, but David still hopes there's a miracle out there that will change his aging mother back into the lively, strong woman of his youth.

"I wish he'd stop bringing those horrible drinks to me—a new one every week—carrot juice, beet juice, who knows what else? He tells me they'll make me strong. I'd rather be weak, I tell him. Just let me drink my tea. That's good enough for me."

David's fears for Anna are so intertwined with his own feelings about aging that he's unconsciously trying to hold back the clock. He's playing overprotective mother, and his mother is reacting just as a child would—with annoyance.

Where's the delicate balance between handling our fears and our parents' needs for autonomy? Unless we want to take over their lives completely and direct their futures for them, we have to know when to back off, when to do what *they allow us to do*. We must know the boundaries of our limited power.

Limited power doesn't mean we allow Mom to hand out $500 to everyone she meets with a good story. Nor do we watch helplessly as she starves because she's afraid to spend money for groceries. We have to weigh each situation, decide what we can do "behind the scenes" to make it better. When Mother's health and welfare are at stake, we step in and do what we have to do.

But as for the rest of that vast gray area between our parent's total independence and our total "taking over," we must come to some mutually acceptable agreement about how far we can go.

When It's Time to Find a Therapist

With all our good intentions, we may still need to bring in an objective third party to help us cope. There are three kinds of therapists, all trained to deal with psychological problems.

1) *Psychiatrists.* They are always M.D.s who have special training in treating emotional and mental problems. If your mother is acting strangely, a psychiatrist will be able to tell if there is a medical reason for her depression or lack of ability to concentrate. What looks like senility is often an older person's reaction to loss and poor health. A psychiatrist, particularly a geriatric psychiatrist, is trained to detect the underlying causes of behavior. To get a list of good psychiatrists in your area, start with your doctor or call the leading medical center in your town for a list of psychiatrists on staff. You can also get in touch with:

> American Psychiatric Association
> 400 K Street N.W.
> Washington, DC 20005
> Phone: 202-682-6000
> Website: www.psych.org
> E-mail: APA@psych.org

2) *Clinical psychologists.* These professionals also have training in clinical diagnosis, so they can pick up on changes in your parent's cognitive abilities. They may or may not have a Ph.D. in psychology, and they often specialize in specific age groups or emotional problems. Ask your doctor for a referral or contact:

> The American Psychological Association
> 750 First Street N.E.
> Washington, DC 20002
> Phone: 202-336-5500
> Website: www.APA.org
> E-mail: membership@APA.org

3) *Clinical social workers.* They have a master's degree and often a Ph.D. in social work. You can find a skilled social worker by checking with your local Family Service agency or United Way office. Many social workers are in private practice (not in a community agency) and under the aegis of a consulting psychiatrist. When this is

the case, your health insurance may cover most or all of the fee. For listings, contact:

> The National Association of Social Workers
> 750 First Street N.E.
> Suite 700
> Washington, DC 20002
> Website: www.socialworkers.org

Therapy, especially long-running therapy, can be expensive. During your first visit, find out from the therapist if his or her services are normally covered by insurance. Then check with your insurance company or agent to find out what your policy covers. Almost all of our states recommend standard reimbursement for psychologists, and less than a third require insurance companies to reimburse patients of social workers. However, if the social worker or psychologist is affiliated with a psychiatrist, you're almost assured of reimbursement from the insurance company. Get the details straight before you embark on therapy.

Many communities offer free or low-cost counseling. To learn what is available for you or your parent, start by calling the mental health department in your city or county.

Once you've selected a therapist, keep in mind that your relationship is not written in stone! It's imperative that you feel at ease with the person. If, after three or four visits, you still feel he or she is talking about someone else, it's likely that you two are not a good match.

When you genuinely like the counselor and feel that he or she is on your wavelength, the scene is set for productive therapy. If your therapist seems to know what you're talking about and projects understanding and compassion, you're on the right path. Don't assume there's "something wrong" with you because you're uncomfortable with the first one or two therapists you try. Just look for someone else until you hit the right combination. It's worth the investment in time and money. You're going to be spending a lot of hours with this individual. Make sure you like him or her!

In this chapter we've focused on how you can cope with your aging parent and still fulfill your own needs. If you want to be a good care-giver and maintain a strong, loving relationship with your parent, you must start by taking care of yourself.

NINE

When Your Parent Has to Move: How to Find the Best Living Arrangements

For some families the answer is separate living quarters for the aging parent. But even though your mother or father is not living with you, you can still play an important role in helping him or her find the right place.

What exists and how do you know if it's right for your parent?

Senior Citizen Buildings

These are government subsidized and are "instant successes" in most areas. Generally, they are attractive, sensibly designed facilities that house a mix of couples and singles. Often there is a social worker, a recreation worker, and sometimes a nurse on the premises. And you will often find a "party room" where residents gather for socializing and programs of all kinds. The waiting lists are generally long.

There are also similar buildings in the private sector. They're set up along the same lines as subsidized housing, but naturally rents are appreciably higher.

Group Homes

About twenty years ago some of the religious and charitable institutions took the lead in providing group homes for their constituents who could no longer cook and do household chores. They are a small, personalized solution for those seniors who are relatively independent but need assistance in daily living. Residents still maintain the independence of maintaining their own room and planning their own social life. Often a nurse comes in each morning to supervise medication and check for health problems. People who live in group homes are usually ambulatory and may even walk to nearby bus lines. Informally, the residents may get together for card games or to hear a lecture. Group homes function almost as residential hotels with the added security of a daily visit from the nurse.

Many group homes have been designed like space-age modules with a center desk where the nurse's station is located and individual rooms radiating out from the center core. They offer a workable combination of independent life with the back-up services and security of a staff on call.

Costs of group homes vary widely, ranging from reasonable to very expensive. In general, those group homes operated by large "umbrella" organizations with long-standing donors can subsidize part of the care from their operating budgets. You may expect to pay about $1500 to $3000 per month.

Retirement Communities

This kind of living arrangement is set up so that totally independent people live separately from those who need more supervision and help. Once your parent moves into a "full service" retirement community, usually in a warm climate such as Arizona or Florida, he or she will be cared for no matter what the future brings. With luck, he may stay in his independent apartment until he dies. Or, if his health and cognitive powers start to deteriorate, he will move to a part of the facility that offers more care.

The advantages of retirement communities are obvious—attractive individual homes or apartments set in a planned community with golf courses, swimming pools, recreation halls, meeting rooms, a variety of classes offered at nominal costs, plenty of neighbors with whom to socialize. The Del Webb corporation developments, notably the Sun City group in the Phoenix area, are an example of this kind of senior living.

The disadvantages? Do your parents want to live in a community where they socialize with the same people all the time? How do they feel about living around a single-age population—no children unless they're visiting grandparents, none of the stimulation generated by the differences between the generations?

In a nutshell, making this kind of decision means you and your parents have to evaluate what is most important for all of you. If your Mom and Dad think nothing of hopping a commuter train or driving downtown to hear a jazz concert or seek out the newest Ethiopian restaurant, they may not be ready for this kind of living.

Again, costs vary widely. Since senior living facilities are now big business, the costs depend on the area (lower in small towns in the non-typical retirement areas and higher in places facing the ocean in Florida). Since many retirement communities are in warm climates, prospective residents can gauge the typical cost by contacting a state Chamber of Commerce or checking directly with the real estate corporations. It's difficult to name even a ballpark figure since the area of the country and the kinds of facilities available (spas, tennis courts, etc.) will dictate the price.

Retirement Hotels

The retirement hotel is one of the best solutions for a large segment of older people. They are located in the same cities and towns where your parents may have lived their entire lives. There is a retirement hotel not far from the University of Chicago in Chicago's Hyde Park neighborhood which offers the "best of all possible worlds" for its inhabitants. This facility was started by the Episcopal Diocese but is non-sectarian. The residents move in when they can no longer keep up their home or apartment but still want to live in this cultural beehive in the city. There is no typical occupant other than the bond that most of them have lived in this neighborhood for many years.

They are retired college professors, postal workers, small business owners. Like the neighborhood around it, the hotel is an integrated community with a healthy mix of all races and lifestyles: married couples, singles, friends living together.

In this pleasant situation, residents work with the activity director to select what they would like—from bridge lessons to foreign-language films. Those who drive keep their car in a nearby garage, and there are vans for trips to supermarkets and the like.

One resident remarks, "You are not lonesome here. You can participate with peers as much or as little as you like. We all have dinner together in the dining room, since the evening meal is included as part of our rent. But you can come and go as you wish, simply sitting down at a table that's available."

This facility is a kind of model for retirement hotels in that it provides two levels of assistance. There is always a nurse on call for the apartment dwellers, and in the event that a resident's general condition becomes markedly worse or he or she develops Alzheimer's, that resident can move to another floor where there is complete care. As in other facilities, costs vary according to the services offered and the area of the country.

Assisted Living

Assisted living facilities are springing up rapidly all over the country and are profit-making businesses. Many of them are run by huge corporations that have caught onto the reality of the rapidly "graying of America." They can range from top-notch right down the ladder to marginal. Up to now there has been very little government regulation of these facilities, but more and more states are passing regulatory measures that will guarantee a code of standards.

The Assisted Living Federation of America is an umbrella group for this proliferating business. They report that, by and large, assisted living residences serve senior people, both men and women, with an average age of 83, who can no longer live alone or often do not wish to be on their own any longer.

What does it cost? The variation here is enormous, ranging from the "average" $76 per day fee, figured by the Assisted Living Federation in a survey of some of its member facilities, and going both appreciably up and down from there. Since the concept of assisted living is a relatively new one, having emerged on the senior housing scene about ten years ago, facilities vary widely in services provided and rates charged. In the same survey by the Federation, assisted living residences were charging from $24 per day up to $206 per day.

Can the government help you bear the financial burden? Actually, not much. Some state and local governments offer subsidies for low-income residents and some residences do offer limited financial assistance. Many families find that this is the time when an individual's long-term health insurance coverage comes in very handy.

What services are provided? In the typical assisted living facility your parent can expect to receive the following:

- Three meals a day, served in a common dining room with accommodation for special diets—diet management for people with diabetes, colitis, or high blood pressure and related ailments that require a low-salt diet
- Housekeeping and linen services
- Transportation to medical care, shopping, and community services
- Assistance with bathing, dressing, eating, toileting, walking
- 24-hour security
- Emergency call system in each housing unit
- Access to emergency medical care
- Access to opthalmologists and audiologists
- Medication management
- Social and recreational activities
- Exercise and wellness programs, including physical therapy
- Frequent check-ups by podiatrist, especially useful for elderly people who cannot cut their own toenails and by those requiring orthopedic shoes with special modifications
- Therapy and pharmacy services
- Special needs programs for residents with Alzheimer's disease or dementia as well as post-stroke and Parkinson's Disease sufferers and others who need help with walking

"The test of a people is how it behaves toward the old" is a quote from a famous rabbi named Abraham Joshua Heschel. This universal truth applies to all cultures in all eras. In our youth-oriented culture it's really not fashionable to be "old." "Old" can mean "out of it," not really in the mainstream, a sort of leftover from another age, an unimportant, irrelevant reminder of a far-away time. But, luckily for us and our aging parents, more and more individuals and institutions have stopped stereotyping seniors and started to respect and relate to this age group on a person-by-person basis.

In every community you will find oases of love and commitment. One such is the Gidwitz Place for Assisted Living in Deerfield, Illinois, which is operated by the Council for Jewish Elderly. With adequate funding from this private social service agency, Gidwitz Place is a demonstration project, a model for what an assisted living facility should be. The average age is 86.

About 25 percent of the residents are men, either living in an apartment unit with their wives or on their own. In many such facilities men feel overwhelmed by the preponderance of women and tend to hole up in their own apartments, emerging only for exercise sessions or meals. But Mary Ann Manion, director of Gidwitz Place, is an innovator. She started a kind of "Boys' Club" with a clubhouse—a separate lounge with television sets tuned to the latest sports—a refrigerator for beer if they want it, and an active social life outside the facility with frequent trips to sports and other events.

Gidwitz residents who are able to are encouraged to volunteer. One charming woman handles mail distribution, others volunteer in the building's well-stocked library. Frequently, residents from Gidwitz Place volunteer at a food pantry in Chicago, especially at Christmas and other holidays where they gain by "giving back" to others less fortunate. Their lives are full and actively engaged with a great deal of family involvement. Often, family members come for Friday night dinner and can reserve a private dining room for a family event. The atmosphere is lively, with many organized activities, even high school reunions for those who attended the same high school in their early days in Chicago.

Assisted living is definitely here to stay and will only grow as the proportion of the "old-elderly" cohort increases. When one reaches 85 years, he or she is considered part of this population by demographers. This age group is projected to increase 33.2 percent between the years 2000 and 2010. Consider that the U.S. Bureau of the Census says that in 1990 they represented around 3.1 million of our population. In the year 2000 that number jumped to 4.25 million, and in 2010 the projection is for more than 5.6 million men and women 85 and older.

For more information on assisted living across the country, contact:

Assisted Living Facilities Federation of America
10300 Eaton Place
Suite 400
Fairfax, VA 22030
Phone: 703-691-8100
Website: www.ALFA.org

Nursing Homes

Nobody is beating on the door to get into a nursing home, no matter how excellent it is. But if your parent is growing frail, has been diagnosed as having severe dementia or Alzheimer's, or has chronic health problems such emphysema, advanced heart disease, or is suffering the debility of a serious stroke, a nursing home may be the best solution. Your concern is to find the right one for your parent.

Start by asking physicians, nurses, geriatric social workers, and friends. Your local council on aging or county senior citizen department will have a list of recommended nursing homes. Quite often, the best nursing homes are run by philanthropic or religious institutions. These not-for-profit homes have to conform to all state regulations but generally have a more personal "feel."

Visit a variety of facilities and take a careful look:

- Is it clean?
- Is the food interesting? Is there a dietitian who plans the menus?
- How many aides are on staff? Are they pleasant, well-informed and caring?
- Is there a physician on staff? If so, with which hospital is he connected? Do a dentist and a podiatrist check the residents periodically?
- How does the place feel to you? Is everyone sitting around staring at the floor or is there a lively mix of activity?
- Do you get a sense that residents are routinely given drugs to make them compliant and less trouble to the staff?

- Did you visit this facility without advance warning and did you visit it at different times during the day? Paying a surprise visit is an excellent way to assess the place.
- Are there interesting programs and ways for your parents to socialize?
- Do you feel the staff genuinely treats the people as individuals or is there a sterile by-the-numbers atmosphere?

The way the facility impresses you is the most important part of the selection process. If you get a sense of warmth and caring, a feeling that this is not a storehouse where people wait for death but an ongoing, viable facility where each day of life is celebrated, then this is the best alternative.

In selecting a nursing home it's the subtle feel of the place that really tells the story. Jim and Martha Anderson have this to say about their experiences with nursing homes. Jim relates:

"When Martha's mother suffered an encompassing stroke that took her from an active woman with a good golf handicap and a busy social life to a weak, frail "older woman," we knew she needed full-time care. And her doctor did too. Martha is an only child so we had to make the decisions. We chose a nursing home we knew about—state-of-the-art place with beautiful grounds and single rooms.

"After her mother had been in there for two months, we realized that she was desperately lonely. Staying in her room most of the time and really not having any conversations beyond a chat or two with the floor nurses was affecting her negatively. We had a long talk with her, and she surprised us by asking about another home she knew about. We took a look at it and were not impressed—a small facility with all the patients housed in double or triple rooms. I was ready to turn it down immediately.

"But Martha insisted we take Mom over to see this place. We had a tough time transporting her, wheelchair and all, but we made it. My mother-in-law sat in on an orientation meeting with the director, and several times during the conversation I saw her smile and look more animated than we had seen in months. Amazingly, she didn't mind sharing a room. Her potential roommate was a lively little woman who was just as physically challenged as our Mom but a busy bee. She was organizing a handicraft exhibition that week and showed us how the rehabilitation therapist had helped her learn to crochet again after a stroke.

"This place was, for want of a better word, homey. The director was a real people person. She was free with smiles and hugs. It wasn't fancy. It lacked the elegance of the first nursing home. But we moved Mom in there anyway. She likes it. It's the best thing we could have done for her."

Twenty to thirty years ago, bad nursing homes made for volumes of newspaper and television exposes—and in many cases, justly so. Happily, the picture has changed, partly because of this public spotlight. With the growth of the advocacy movement in all segments of life, Americans have become better consumers. They ask more questions. They demand more answers. By and large nursing homes where abuses had taken place have been forced out of business. There have always been good nursing homes, staffed by people who care and genuinely like working with the elderly. But those "bad apples" certainly gave nursing homes a bad name and engendered more watchdog activity.

Sharon Jarchin, president of Sharon Jarchin Health Care Marketing in Huntington, New York, represents Intercounty Health Facilities Association, an organization of 59 nursing homes on Long Island. She emphasizes that the state of New York has some of the most stringent regulations in the nation and encourages children of aging parents to check out any facility through a variety of means—personal visits, of course; recommendations from friends; and careful searching on the Internet in your area.

Ms. Jarchin advises families who are considering a nursing home for their parent not to go in with preconceived ideas: "Family members should not feel that nursing home placement is a terrible alternative or the last resort. Thorough research and finding the right facility can often benefit the resident so that they are in a safe and caring environment, offering the care-givers some respite from the responsibility and worry so often associated with caring for an aging parent."

Alzheimer's Units

How do you know when your parent's behavior may indicate the onset of Alzheimer's or a related dementia condition? Mrs. Hazel Childs, Director of Family Services at the Wealshire facility, located in Lincolnshire, Illinois, offers some helpful clues:

- How does your parent look? Is she appreciably thinner than she was or has she gained a large amount of weight lately? Both conditions can be symptoms of Mother's inability to remember whether or not she has eaten that day. The abnormal loss of weight naturally is tied to her forgetting to eat, perhaps just brewing a cup of tea several times a day. The obese parent (who is blessed with a hearty appetite) may honestly feel she did not have breakfast even though it was twenty minutes ago.
- Look in the refrigerator. Are all those nicely packaged individual meals you bring over still sitting just where you left them?
- Is the clutter increasing in the house?
- Is your mother or father keeping up with the bills? Are the figures accurate in the checkbook or have several transactions been made and not recorded? You can check that against the register to see if all checks were written down.
- How is your parent's general appearance? When a former fashion plate is walking around in mismatched socks and a nightgown hanging down from an incorrectly buttoned sweater, this can mean any number of things—ranging from anger at becoming old to depression to a signal that cognitive abilities are slipping.
- How is your parent's facial expression? Is he no longer animated? Is he staying away from things he used to do? Is his general tone "flat"? This flatness, or lack of affect, can signify either a severe depression or an actual early sign of an Alzheimer's type condition.
- Have you noticed that your father has a difficult time with visual judgments? Did you get him new glasses, yet he still seems tentative about moving from one area to another? People with Alzheimer's disease begin to lose visual perception. They may stop at the edge of a rug because they are not sure whether they have to step up to move onto that rug. At Wealshire all changing physical

dimensions are clearly and brightly marked. For example, each dining table has a white cloth and brightly colored plates so that residents can distinguish between the table top and the plate.

Hazel Childs and other experts in this field recommend an important next step—a visit to a geriatric neurologist. Wealshire, like some other Alzeheimer's facilities across the country, also operates a memory clinic under the direction of a neurologist. The assessment sessions at a memory clinic are usually covered by Medicare and supplemental insurance plans. This step is an imperative one because lay people, especially the children of aging parents, simply lack the tools to distinguish between what looks like eccentric behavior and real cognitive changes.

What will it be like for your parent in an Alzheimer's unit? Most people move into a facility from having lived independently. It's a difficult adjustment. Think of it, in a more extreme way of course, as your first days away from home in a college dorm. It's noisier simply because of the number of people now surrounding you. You don't know any of these people, and, more importantly, they don't know how wonderful you are. Familiar cues are gone. It takes time to adjust.

Don't expect your parents to thank you for engineering this move, but as time goes on, you will notice subtle changes. The "tea party ladies," as Mrs. Childs calls them, never lose their social skills. They enjoy conversing with others and taking part in activities. For many, this may be the first time they have socialized in several months. They were too occupied with just trying to manage daily living on their own as well as covering up their losses in front of other people.

The staff at Wealshire recommends keeping up your former visiting schedule. If you always took Mom out to lunch on Wednesday and dropped over on an occasional weekend evening, then continue doing that.

Other tips for visiting:

- Don't visit in Mom's room. Walk out to the refreshment area or walk outside if the weather permits it. Make it a little special occasion.
- Don't ask Mom what she had for lunch. That's the kind of last ditch conversation that tips Mom off to the fact that you are uneasy and can't think of what to say.

- Bring something to show and share—a magazine with brightly colored photographs of special recipes, the local paper, a photo album.
- Make sure the younger generations in your family visit and visit often. Mom may have forgotten their birthdays or even her own, but their young faces and fresh new conversation is truly "good medicine" for her.

Watching one's parent lose his abilities is one of the most painful experiences adult children have to endure. But diminished cognitive ability is sometimes a fact of life in our rapidly growing "old-elderly" population segment. By the time a person reaches 85 years of age, he or she has a 49 percent chance of developing dementia or a related disorder. What can you do to ease this situation?

Your first task is take the responsibility of finding the correct placement for your parent unless you decide to keep him or her at your home. It's also of paramount importance that you find a geriatric neurological specialist who understands what is happening and what you can do to help. Finally, you will have to balance your parent's needs and your own.

An excellent facility like Wealshire can run up to $60,000 to $100,000 a year, depending on your part of the country. If your parent has long-term health care insurance, that may cover a portion of the costs. Can your siblings help with the rest? Is there a non-profit facility, often funded through a religious or philanthropic association, in your area?

To get started in your search for the right place, try the following:

> Alzheimer's Association
> 919 N. Michigan Avenue
> Suite 1000
> Chicago, IL 60611-1676
> Phone: 1-800-272-3900
> Website: www.Alz.org

Geriatric Care Managers

This national organization is a private group that represents geriatric care managers (usually social workers or nurses) who specialize in caring for the elderly. They are experienced in working not only with you but with your parent's doctor, attorney, or trust officer to help coordinate his or her care. Fees range from $80 to $100 per hour. Medicare does not cover the costs of this service.

Erica Karp, director of Northshore Eldercare Management in Evanston, Illinois, became a geriatric care manager several years ago when the category was almost non-existent in any formal sense. As a therapist she was seeing so many families with the problem of what to do with a failing parent that she began to specialize in this field. Mrs. Karp says, "It's important to involve the parent at his or her level of capability. Some people are capable of deciding for themselves. The children can offer two or three choices and bring the parent into the decision. For parents not able to make that kind of decision, the adult child can pick the facility but then bring the parent into the decision about what color she would like the walls to be painted or which furniture and personal belongings should be moved to the new living place."

Karp points out that, "Everyone in the family going through this difficult time needs emotional support. A care manager can give the family methods of approaching the subject. Sometimes it works better if the care manager is 'the heavy,' the one who says, 'This has to be done.'"

For information in this area, contact:

Geriatric Care Managers
1604 N. Country Club Road
Tucson, AZ 85716
Phone: 520-881-8008
Website: www.caremanager.org

For your own physical and emotional health as well as the well-being of your parent, it's essential to "do your homework." Research the help that is available to you to ensure the best possible solution. And, most important of all, before you arrange any permanent move, visit, visit, visit, and trust your feelings about the way a place "feels" to you and your parent.

What Do I Do When My Parent Lives 2500 Miles Away?

This dilemma is a fairly common one these days, with families living thousands of miles away from each other. There are an estimated 7 million care-givers trying to do the job via long distance. And as Americans live longer than ever before, the problem will only increase. The typical long-distance care-giver is a Baby Boomer who left home either for college or for the dream job that beckoned her or him across the country. Is it easy? Unless you are one of those "head in the sand" adult children, long-distance care can be one of the most difficult tasks you will ever have to face.

When you sense that your parent needs more help than he's getting now, the sense of guilt and helplessness you feel can overwhelm you. Start by realizing that you alone cannot handle this situation. Fortunately, as the phenomenon of the long-distance care-giver developed, so did a variety of support services.

If you work for a large company, check with your human relations department. Many companies offer support groups and counseling for employees in this difficult situation.

Find out if your company offers unpaid leave to deal with this kind of family problem. In 1993 Congress passed the Family and Medical Leave Act, which guarantees eligible employees the right to be off the job for a maximum of 12 weeks without pay. Within that time, an adult child of an aging parent can assess the situation and look for alternatives.

If you are unable to take that amount of time away from your job, you can start the process of finding the right help through bona fide professional organizations set up to deal with the long-distance care-giver. You will save countless hours and plenty of telephone and Internet frustration if you start with the Eldercare Locator. This is a free nationwide directory assistance service, a hotline for everything from finding a good Meals on Wheels program for your parents to home health care, home health observation, and elder abuse prevention, among many other programs. To reach them, just call:

202-296-8130

The Eldercare Locator is a project of the National Association of Area Agencies on Aging:

Phone: 800-677-1116
Website: www.aoa.dhhs.gov

You will find both sources very helpful. They prefer to handle questions and referrals with you on the telephone.

Again, for long-distance care, you will find Geriatric Care Managers (listed above) a goldmine of information. A geriatric care manager will provide an assessment of physical and mental problems and will help you locate the program and/or facility your parent needs.

Managing from a distance takes enormous persistence. Once you determine the kind of help your parents need, it's imperative to travel to their location as soon as possible. The complaints against the home health care worker you might be hearing on a weekly basis may or may not be founded in fact. After you have done your homework and located the right help and/or the right place to live, there is only one way to resolve the situation—in person.

TEN

How to Talk About Difficult Subjects

We all reach a point where the unthinkable must be thought, and our silent fears and apprehensions must be dealt with openly.

In this chapter we're going to discuss ways of talking to our parents about some thorny issues: remarriage, finances, turning over responsibility to us, giving up their driver's license, moving out of their home, failing powers, illness, and death.

Our parents may be dropping subtle hints or ascribing their own circumstances to other people—"Mrs. Smith isn't driving any more. She couldn't stay in her lane." This is their buttoned-up generation's way of indirectly letting us know that they're encountering new problems as they age. On the other hand, they may pretend that everything is wonderful, the same as it always was—yet they're silently seething because we're not addressing their problems.

It's up to us to make the first move, to broach uncomfortable subjects.

How? We must take off our blinders and face the issues we hoped we'd never have to face. The *way* we talk about the issues is important. It can spell the difference between creating hurt feelings and ill will between us or serving as a positive stepping-stone to the next phase of our relationship.

Talk Nice!

Use those effective ego-syntonic words we talked about in the chapters on communication. You may have to say heavy-duty things—the kinds of things you hoped never to have to mention. But by your words and the genuine caring that goes with them, you can help soften the blow.

Get rid of platitudes. Nobody who's facing illness and the infirmities of old age wants to be told, "Everything's great! You're just making a mountain out of a molehill." A case in point:

Edna Conray, 80, is suffering from emphysema. Her condition has worsened in the last year, and she now must have oxygen with her at all times. Recently, she was invited to a high school graduation party for her grandson Greg. He's the baby of all the grandchildren and one of her favorites.

"You're coming, of course," her daughter Susan announced with a "we won't take no for an answer" tone.

Edna thought of the embarrassment of dragging along the oxygen tanks. People always stared so. She hated to go out in public any more. "We'll see," she said.

"Now, mother. You're just being silly. You're fine. And being at the party will do you good."

Edna knew she wasn't "fine" and she resented her daughter for what she interpreted as "making light of my condition." She made up her mind. There was no arguing with her bull-headed girl. When the time came, she'd simply mail Greg a check and tell them she was too ill to go to the party.

How could her daughter Susan handle it so that her mother could "save face" and still be a part of this meaningful family occasion? She might have said something like this: "Mom, I know you're embarrassed by the oxygen unit. It's uncomfortable for you. I understand that. But the whole family will be there to honor Greg. He wants you there. You know how he feels about you. Could you really give it some thought? Maybe when you weigh the joy of sharing this day with Greg and the rest of us against having to be there with oxygen tanks, you'll decide to take a chance and come to the party."

This kind of message helps assure Edna that she's cared for and that her presence is important, that she still has a function in the family. It's also telling her that if she finds the courage to go out in public with oxygen this time, she'll be able to do it again. Susan's words can be kind and loving, but they can keep the responsibility for the decision where it belongs—in her mother's hands. Nobody likes having her mind made up for her. Susan's message can tell her mother, "I know you have health problems now, but you're still in control of these decisions."

Don't patronize. Your mother may be getting older, and she may have great physical and emotional difficulties, but she is not a baby! Do not adopt the editorial "we," as in "are we ready for our bath now?"

Margo Collingsworth, 89, was a *grande dame* of her time. Until the day she broke her hip, she still managed to get herself to the Friday afternoon concert at Symphony Center, where her family had maintained box seats since she was a little girl.

The broken hip did not mend well, and she found herself in the hospital for several weeks. Besides the indignities of standard hospital routine, in which her bodily functions were suddenly a major topic of conversation, she particularly resented the pseudo-cheerful nurses.

One young nurse, who was recently transferred to her floor, popped in one morning with a "Good morning, Granny. Did we use the bathroom this morning?"

This was more than Margo could stand. Summoning all her strength, she informed the nurse, "I am not your Granny. I am Mrs. Collingsworth. And as far as I remember, we did not meet in the bathroom this morning. I don't know about your use of the bathroom, but if you'd like to know about mine, just ask me."

Don't compare your parent with someone else. "Look at Uncle Joe. He's in worse shape than you." Or "You have a lot to be grateful for. You can still walk." When we try to "make light" of their afflictions in this way, our parents think we're invalidating them. It's as if we're saying, "What's happening to you is not important. And my judgment about your condition is much better than yours."

We'd do better to acknowledge our parents' physical and emotional ailments and go on from there. We can say something like, "I know it's hard for you now that you're alone. But remember, I still care. I'm here for you. I'll listen when you want to talk."

Now let's look at some specific problems with a high "discomfort index" and find out how we might talk about them.

When Not to Report a Relative's Illness to Our Parents

This subject is tricky. When a distant relative dies, do we let Mom know about it? Do we tell our aging father in the nursing home that his old pal Mac is so ill he can no longer visit? Do we tell them about our own health problems?

In each case, we have to make a judgment call. We can decide whether to tell or not tell by evaluating the amount of pain each decision would bring. For instance, is this a condition that can only get worse, such as a fatal disease? If it's not, then perhaps we can wait until the situation stabilizes. For example, your cousin in South Dakota has a serious heart attack followed by bypass surgery. He used to call your father once a week and frequently made stops to see him when he was traveling on business. Now cousin James will be laid up for two to three months. It will probably be a few weeks before he can even call Dad. What do you do?

If you honestly think Dad is not strong enough to handle the news, then tell only part of the truth. Explain that James is hospitalized with back problems and he'll be in touch as soon as he's well enough. "Back problems" are more easily accepted than a serious heart attack, and James's hospitalization excuses him from being in touch. If you say nothing, Dad will be hurt by James's sudden withdrawal.

Be aware that you're making the decision for your father by withholding the news. Can you live with that? And will you eventually tell him the truth? What's to be gained by telling Dad about James's health? If it will only worry and upset him, then stick with your original half-truth.

What if a close relative or friend dies? Do you tell your parents? Here again, you can decide on the basis of how much contact your parent has with the relative. When Aunt Mary dies, your mother deserves to know. She'll be immensely hurt when Mary simply stops writing or calling. One yardstick for telling this kind of news is to ask yourself how you would feel if the facts were kept from you.

Giving Up Driving—When Dad Is Creating Panic in the Streets

You know the scenario. You're driving down a two-lane street behind an older person. He's going ten miles under the speed limit. He's hunched up over the wheel peering straight ahead. He can't stay in his lane. From time to time, he slams on the brakes for no apparent reason. He slows down at *every* side street. "He'll never have an accident," you mutter, "he'll just cause them."

Many older people have slow reflexes. They may have impaired vision or hearing. They may have trouble remembering landmarks and street signs. But they won't consider giving up driving. Americans are born knowing they have the rights to life, liberty, the pursuit of happiness, and "wheels" of their own. When an older driver has to give up driving, it's a blow to his independence. For the older man, it means the difference between picking up friends for the Saturday night movie or suffering the indignity of asking for a ride. When he gives up his car, he feels he's "on the shelf."

What do you do when Dad is consistently driving in two lanes or making wide turns that send your heart into your throat? You must decide whether Dad is merely a nuisance or an actual danger on the road. If Dad is drifting into the other lane, slamming on brakes without warning, or generally driving in a hazardous manner, you have to tell him.

It will hurt him, and it will hurt you, too. But you can say something like, "Dad, all your life you've been a safe driver. But now, your driving has changed. You could never forgive yourself if you injured anyone because of your driving. There are more cars on the road now, and driving has become more dangerous. It's time to think about selling the car."

Don't expect him to embrace the idea with enthusiasm. After all, you're taking away an extension of himself. But you have to be insistent, and you can't let him "promise to do better" if he's doing his best right now. Telling a parent that he must stop driving is one of the hardest things we have to do. We're striking at his sense of self;

we're putting him into a new position that he doesn't wish to assume. This is one of those "it's a tough job, but somebody has to do it" situations. And we don't have a choice.

Enlist Your Parent's Doctor in Your Cause

If your mother is one of those people who believes "nobody cleans as well as I do" and is known far and wide as "crazy clean" Judith, you can sympathize with Laura Ambett. She says, "It's heartbreaking to see my mother wearing spotted clothing and cooking with dirty utensils. She was always so immaculate. When my sisters and I broach the subject of cleaning help, she flies into a rage. We're afraid she'll have a heart attack, so we back down."

Or consider Don Pritchard's problem. He says, "My father insists on going outside during the winter without overshoes. He still wears the leather-soled dress shoes he favored in his youth. He's already fallen on ice three times. Through sheer luck he hasn't broken a hip. But next time?"

Remember, *it's okay to intervene when it's a question of your parent's health and welfare.* There *are* situations that require an "end run" around Mother and Dad. First go to your strongest ally—your parent's doctor. A doctor with elderly patients has been this route many times before. He'll be prepared to back up the adult children because it's in the best interest of his patient. When "crazy clean" Etta comes in for her check-up next month, he'll tell her, "Your daughter tells me she wants to get some help in the house. I agree with her. That way you'll be able to stay in your own place. It's your choice, Etta. If you can't tolerate household help, you'll have to consider giving up your apartment."

And certainly Don Pritchard's father will get an earful from his doctor at the next visit. After a briefing from Don, the doctor will present the senior Mr. Pritchard with a similar ultimatum: "Either wear boots when you go outside or I'll talk to your son about hiring a companion for you."

In almost all families, when the mother or father reaches a point of not being able to cope totally alone, the "kids" step in to help. Sanford Finkel, M.D., a geriatric psychiatrist, is an expert on the elderly and their family relationships. More than thirty years ago he ran one of the first therapy groups for older people. Dr. Finkel says, "It's a myth that kids don't take care of their elderly parents. Not only do they worry about them and try to plan for their welfare but they spend an average of 12 hours a week tending to them."

Talking About Money Matters

At several points in this book, we've mentioned the importance of having access to your parent's funds. If you can't sign checks or get into the safe deposit box, all sorts of costly and frustrating complications may arise. When trust and closeness is built up over time and your parent has learned to share this function with you, you're able to act in a crisis.

Some parents, however, interpret your very real need to be involved with their finances as intrusion and, worse, a gambit to take away their independence. Your job is to allay their fears; explain that you don't intend to take over their lives. Stick to "what ifs"—what if Dad is still in Florida for the winter and his household insurance bill needs to be paid? What if he or Mom end up in the hospital and aren't well enough to sign their checks? Nobody likes to talk about vulnerability and all the bad "what ifs" that can happen. But if we don't talk about it now, when they're in control of their physical and emotional powers, it can be devastating later.

And some parents refuse to listen to any talk of financial planning. One son whose mother lives in Louisville, Kentucky, says, "My mother covers her ears when I try to talk to her about money. Once I found unpaid bills tucked behind the flour canister in the kitchen. When I go home to visit, I know my blood pressure is going to jump fifteen points at least. That house is a warren of loose pieces of paper, cancelled checks, bills, my mother's old love letters, you name it. She's a delightful, charming lady. And if something happens to her, I'll have to hire three lawyers to straighten out the mess."

This son is well-off financially, so he can afford to be cavalier about his mother's refusal to face her financial situation. Most of us don't have that luxury.

If Mom "covers her ears" when you try to talk about money, you have to point out that her money can go quickly if illness strikes. And her care will become a hardship on you and your brothers and sisters.

You can take several steps to get a handle on your parent's financial picture and plan for her future:

1) Sit down with Mom and find out how much is in savings, what kind of interest she's getting on her account, the amount of her monthly Social Security check, her insurance coverage, and so on.

2) After you've totaled all her assets, come up with a realistic assessment of living expenses. Is Mom's cash outlay too high in proportion to her holdings? Certainly, we're not suggesting you grill her as to how much she spends in the local grocery store or beauty shop. But if, for example, she's paying exorbitant rent, you can point out how moving to a less-expensive apartment will assure her of more future financial security.

3) What is her health insurance situation? If Mom has not been hospitalized or ill in some time, she may assume "Medicare will cover everything." It doesn't.

Medicare is designed to help an over-65 person pay doctor and hospital bills, but *it does not provide complete coverage.* If your parent is unfortunate enough to require a lengthy hospital stay, he or she may end up with bills totaling several thousand dollars for services not covered by Medicare. That's why it's essential to understand your parent's coverage and take steps to purchase supplemental insurance or enroll in a Medicare HMO.

Medicare consists of two programs:

1) *Hospital Insurance (Part A).* This provides partial coverage, usually the major portion of a hospital visit, but an extended hospital stay is not completely covered. It's wise to be aware of the various coverage regulations and how they apply to your parent's situation. If you are uncertain about the details, ask the hospital for an appointment with their social worker or a patient services representative who can spell out the stipulations.

Other provisions are made for care in a skilled nursing facility (aftercare following a stroke or broken hip, for example). But Medicare does not cover care for someone with a chronic condition such as Alzheimer's disease.

2) *Medical Insurance (Part B)*. Medicare pays 80 percent of the covered costs of physicians' services, outpatient hospital services, outpatient physical therapy, and visiting nurse services. Your parent pays the difference plus the deductible. Part B does not cover charges Medicare considers excessive. For instance, if your doctor charges $400 for an operation but the Medicare-approved amount is $300, Medicare will only pay 80 percent of the $300.

For a complete rundown on Medicare benefits (which are subject to year-to-year change), call your local Social Security office and request a copy of "Medicare and You." You can also get a booklet on "How to Fill Out a Medicare Claim Form," which will guide you through the process of filling out the "Patient's Request for Medicare Payment" form.

Once you understand exactly what Medicare does and does not pay, you'll be knowledgeable when shopping for what's called "Medigap" health insurance—policies that are designed to cover most or all of the expenses Medicare doesn't pay. It is also advisable to look into Medicare HMOs that are available in your area.

The important thing is to act before Mom or Dad becomes ill and you're all caught without enough coverage. Talking about eventual illness and debility isn't pleasant at any time, but you can point out what would happen should sudden illness strike when you are not financially prepared.

How do you talk about the grim possibilities?

1) *Be prepared for resistance from some parents.* Some older people, just like some younger people, dislike discussing reality. Be patient, listen to their point of view, but gently stick to your guns. Illness is an issue you must talk about, and there's no better time than the present.

2) *Use "I" statements.* "Dad, I'm concerned about your future. Maybe I'm a worrywart, but please hear me out."

3) *Remember you're breaking ground.* Intimate, meaningful discussion establishes a habit of shared communication. This will make it easier to handle new problems whenever they erupt.

What? You're Marrying Him!

Americans are living longer, and remarriage is more common. When our parents remarry, there are certain issues that must be brought out, painful, embarrassing, discomforting issues. What about the prenuptial agreement? If Mom has a house, will she continue to keep it in her own name? Will her new husband include her in his insurance policy? Is his pension big enough to take care of both of them? Will she contribute to the family expenses? What are the terms of both their wills? Who has power of attorney if mother's mate should become ill? Who'll pay the rent?

Your parent and his or her intended mate are entering a relationship with many social, emotional, and financial entanglements. So first sit down with your mother and have a frank discussion about finances. Ask her, "Is John able to pay living expenses?" "Are you expecting to kick in? If so, how much a month will you contribute?"

Your position here is to protect your mother or father so they are not left destitute upon the death of the new mate. If Mom has decided to contribute her monthly Social Security check to the new marriage, then you must encourage her to hold onto other assets: "Mom, it's imperative to keep your stocks and house title in your own name. These are what guarantee your independence. If something happens to John, I know you don't want to be without resources." Say it as calmly and non-emotionally as you can. But say it. This is reality talk. The bride-to-be may prefer not to sully happy days with brass-tacks talk about money. But it's your responsibility to point out *her responsibility to herself and her family.*

Next, you may decide to call a meeting with your mother's intended and his children. If you're uncomfortable with doing this (and you will be!), it's a good idea to bring in your family lawyer and suggest that the other family do the same. That way, both lawyers can work to protect the interests of their respective clients. You'll have an objective third party representing you. And it's better to do this now than wait until a crisis develops and you have to barge into an ongoing situation.

If Mom and her new husband are having difficulties adjusting to each other, remember that you're not a marriage counselor. It's not your job to interfere *unless you see that your mother or father is not being cared for properly.* If the new member of the family is bilking your parent of all her savings or penny-pinching to the degree that Mother's health is affected, you not only have the right but the duty to talk about it—fast.

Occasionally in remarriages among seniors, one mate will be jealous of his spouse's close relationship with her children. Typically, this happens when a man with no children or one who has only a distant relationship with his own kids marries into a close, loving family. He feels like an interloper. He never knows the punch line to any of the family stories. Nor is he comfortable with the kidding and teasing that goes on among your family members.

He may respond by deciding to move his new wife half-way across the country. Or he may set up their social life so that your mother no longer has free time to spend with you. When this happens, it's up to you to maintain closeness. You'll have to persist if you want to keep the relationship going. Of course, you'll want to avoid disturbing their privacy, but when you sense you're being shut out, start talking!

Simply state your case: "John, I know you and Mom are busy and have a lot of friends. But we want to spend time with Mom, too. So I will continue to make plans with Mom for times when we can be together." Then follow through. If Mom likes to shop, take her to the shopping center when John is playing poker or staying home watching TV. You'll be doing her a favor by making plans. She may be feeling guilty about leaving John for an hour or two, but if you set it up, you've relieved her of trying to satisfy both her kids and her new husband.

When you're dealing with a resentful "step-parent," it's best to state your terms tactfully. Make sure you don't put your mother in the middle of a sparring match. It's important not to diminish his status or appear as a threat to your new "Dad." Try to get him to see that there's room in Mom's life for all of you.

In fact, you have yet another course available that might make Mom more comfortable and draw your new relative into the family circle. Make time to be alone with him. Meet him for lunch, call him sometimes and make it clear that you want to talk to him, get to know him better. Once he gets over his initial reserve, he'll appreciate your efforts. There's nothing as flattering as being pursued for oneself. John will feel a warm spot for the kid who looks upon him as a worthwhile individual, not just "my mother's husband." Little by little, you can melt him until he actually begins to enjoy the family gatherings.

No, Mom, You Can't Come to Live with Us

There is no more painful, unhappy time than when your parent begins to lose abilities and he or she can no longer live alone. If you and your parent can afford an additional $100 to $150 per day (in urban areas), you can always opt for a companion. To find a companion, you may call a local home-help agency (bonded agencies are listed as such), your local hospital, or even a city program that trains people to be "homemaker helpers."

But what if you don't have that amount of money to spend? And what if Mom really prefers to come and live with you? And what if, after long deliberation, you've decided that you can't handle it?

You have to face the music. You might tell her directly, and *without apologizing,* that you're away from home all day at your job or there are too many stairs in your house or you'd all be too crowded. And if you really want to strengthen your case, tell her that your husband (or wife) is simply too overworked or nervous to handle another person living in your home. No matter what you say, the parent who wants to come and live with you is going to resent it.

Your best recourse is to say what needs to be said immediately, to say it gently, and to stick to your story. If you keep embellishing, adding more reasons why she can't move in, you've only added "sniveling coward" to your list of attributes. Decide what you want to give as a reason, or reasons, and then repeat it when necessary. The more you attempt to justify or apologize for your decision, the worse it will be. Depending on your parent's tendency to manipulate you, you'll have many rough days ahead. A parent who's determined to move in will use a variety of techniques to get her way, ranging from temper tantrums to exaggerated claims of helplessness. Be prepared to withstand it all and still keep a sense of proportion.

It helps to speak in an objective manner, as if the two of you were talking about a solution to a project you're both working on.

When you can "step outside yourself" and not let guilt and anger take over, you can be more effective. Talk about stairs or crowding or the fact that she'll be alone most of the time. Stay away from discussions of "you're too high-strung to live with us" or "you know we get along better at a distance" or "there's no kitchen big enough for two women." Why rub salt in the wound?

Carole MacLean, 52, is happily married to Kenneth, a 64-year-old physicist. They married late in life, opted not to have children, and lead busy, productive lives. Carole is a freelance writer with an office in her home. She puts in seven hours a day at the word processor and also volunteers at a church-sponsored day care center one day a week. Kenneth works long hours, so Carole is alone a great deal during the week. Weekends are devoted to socializing with a wide circle of friends.

When Carole's 84-year-old mother fell and broke both arms, the doctor told Carole: "She'll have to have help in the house or move in with you. She can't take care of herself now."

Carole and Kenneth talked it over and decided that Carole should talk to her mother immediately:

"Mom, what do you want to do when you're ready to leave the rehabilitation center?"

Carole's mother said promptly, "Well, you're alone so much of the time, I thought you'd like the company. I won't take up much room! And I can bring Spotty [the cat]. I know you've always been crazy about him."

Carole's heart sank. She hadn't expected that from her independent mother. She shook her head. "No, Mom."

"No? So I'm not wanted. Well, this is a fine thing! It doesn't sound like you talking. Must be that head-in-the-clouds husband of yours."

"It's not just Kenneth. You're going to need a lot of help for quite a while. I can't give up my work. It's very important to me."

"But you work at home!"

"Yes, but you'd be alone most of the time. I'd be in my office with the door shut. It wouldn't be good for you. Much as Kenneth and I love you and would enjoy your company, we can't all live together. I want to keep our relationship with you a good one. And if we're all jammed into that apartment, pretty soon none of us would be happy. Now, if you want to stay in your place, Kenneth and I will help pay for a companion. It's a good solution if you'd rather not move to a nursing home. You think it over and let us know so we can help you make arrangements."

Was Carole's mother satisfied with the decision? Not at first, but when she thought it over, she realized how uncomfortable the situation would be. With Carole and Kenneth helping, she was able to hire a companion for several weeks until she gained mobility. After three months, she remarked to Carole, "I'm so happy I decided not to come and live with you."

Helping Mom or Dad Adjust to a New Home

No matter how we handle the move from a home or apartment of one's own to a group facility, it's an emotionally charged time. We can help ease the move by hanging family pictures in the "new" room, bringing along a comfortable favorite chair and reading light, making sure some familiar objects are nearby. It helps ease the transition and gives the parent some control over her living space. Nothing is more soul-destroying than one of those color-coordinated retirement homes where all the rooms look exactly alike.

The adult children serve as a bridge from the old environment to the new. It's important to visit once or twice a week, and it's vital to take the parent out for lunch or other outings. Otherwise, she feels she's been "dumped" here and you've forgotten about her.

On the other hand, there can be a problem with overly involved children. Sometimes they're so attached that they never give the parent a chance to adjust to her new environment. They take them home every weekend or they visit so often that the older person never gets into the swing of things.

When your parent lives in a retirement home, you're somewhat in the position of the parent who sends her child off to college. If Mom and Dad show up every weekend for the football games or the child is encouraged to return home on weekends, the college kid never quite gets adjusted to dorm life. The young person who never actually starts "living" on campus has really never left home. And with our elderly parents, we have to strike a balance between being accessible and offering support and being so protective that we interfere with acceptance of the new environment.

Can't You Even Say, "Thanks, Kid"?

The task of helping a parent move and adjust is so involved and emotionally draining that we want some recognition for our job. Ideally, we'd like Mom to thank us for bringing her to her new home. So we go to visit her in her new environment; we exclaim enthusiastically about the lovely lounge with its fountain and flowering plants; we gush over the beautiful dining room and the excellent activities program. And Mom says, "It's okay, I guess."

Joanne Karanikis did all the right things before she helped her mother move into a retirement home. She researched carefully, visited several times as all the experts advised, and made sure her mother was well acquainted with not only the facility but some of the people as well. But for every positive thing about the home, her mother had a negative comment. Finally, in desperation, Joanne talked with the social worker:

"My mother doesn't like it here. She keeps complaining that there's nothing to do and she's bored."

The social worker smiled. "Did she tell you that she's vice-president of the sewing circle?"

Joanne was surprised. "No, she never even mentioned it! All she talks about is the boredom and hating the food."

The social worker smiled again. "Did she tell you that she has contributed her recipe for moussaka, and we serve it every two weeks now? It's very popular with the residents. In fact, last Tuesday your mother gave a talk on cooking Greek specialties. She's really participating and becoming quite popular here."

Joanne thought of the sour expression on her mother's face whenever she visited. Tentatively, she asked, "Do you think my mother is acting so dissatisfied for my benefit? Is that possible?"

"Yes, that's entirely possible. She's really enjoying herself, but she won't give you the satisfaction of letting you know that."

Joanne's mother is like a five-year-old who attends his first birthday party. He has a marvelous time playing games and eating all the gooey things we won't let him have at home. When we arrive, he runs toward us and clings as though we had left him forever. He just won't give us the satisfaction of telling us what a great time he had without us. Some of that motivation—a need to get even with us for "deserting" them—can be operating with parents who move to a retirement home. Their ability to keep us off balance with their feigned misery gives them a kind of power. So, to protect ourselves, we need to find out what's really going on, as Joanne did by talking with the social worker. Once you determine that their complaints are unfounded, take your parent's griping with a grain of salt.

Occasionally, however, "where there's smoke, there's fire." Most personnel in retirement facilities and nursing homes are truly dedicated, caring men and women who reap not great financial rewards but emotional gratification from their work. But, as in any job in which the caretaker has control over a powerless charge, a bad apple can sneak in. If your mother or father seems to be afraid of a particular aide or nurse, if you detect unexplained bruises or finger marks on your parent's arm, investigate immediately. In a well-run facility, particularly a private facility, verbal and physical abuse of residents is a rarity. But be alert that it is a possibility.

Talking About Serious Illness and Death

Should your parent become gravely ill, he will need to deal with the stages that accompany all of life's losses—denial, anger, bargaining, depression, and acceptance. And your job is to *permit him to go through these stages of mourning.*

You can't let your fears and anxieties about your parent's impending death keep him from sharing the experience with you.

Wouldn't it be kinder to deny his obvious deterioration and insist that he'll be better soon? Shouldn't we hide the inevitable? Dr. David A. Tomb in his book *Growing Old* points out that if you insist nothing is wrong and he knows the end is near, you run the risk of alienating him at a time when you should be growing closer. Dr. Tomb eloquently describes the deepening relationship of a dying parent and his adult child: "Sad to say, the end of life is often the most productive time for your parent to get to know you, and you him. The intimacy of those last weeks and those last conversations may exceed anything that has gone before."

When your parent is seriously ill, she needs your companionship and support. This is the time when you talk to her about all the meaningful times in her life. She'll feel comforted to hear that "Jimmy is finishing college, after all. He's decided to become a veterinarian. Remember how he brought home all those stray dogs and turtles? Remember how he asked you to knit a sweater for that awful, skinny mutt he found near our garbage?" Talking about shared pleasures in your past reminds your parent of happy times. You shouldn't shy away from those talks.

Some elderly people seem to continue to deny death till the very end. "I'll be better soon, and I'll get out of this hospital," they tell us. If your parent can't face what's obviously happening, then take your cue from him. Let his comments guide what you say to him. If he persists in changing the subject when his condition is mentioned, go along with his denial. But when you sense he may be ready to talk about it, help him by discussing his symptoms, the doctor's opinion, and so on. He may need that impetus to begin gathering himself for what is ahead.

Most parents want to be sure they are leaving the world with their affairs in order. If Mom is saying, "I want Susan to have my pearl ring," don't let your own anxieties about her death keep you from talking about it. Don't try to persuade her, "You're fine, you're not going to die, so don't talk about it." She wants you to listen and assure her that Susan will indeed have Mom's pearl ring.

Many times, neither one of you will know what to say. Just be there. Hold Mom's hand, brush her hair, bring a bouquet of favorite flowers, bake her favorite snack.

When your parent is seriously ill, you too need to grieve. Allow yourself to go through all the emotional reactions that come with mourning. And at the same time, take care of yourself. Let other family members and friends help you now. Feeling part of the family of man is an important part of your healing. It's not wrong to be with family and friends, to laugh, to enjoy a meal at a new restaurant. In the midst of this sad, difficult period, it's normal and healthy to seek life-affirming experiences and human contact. It's the way you carry on the torch from your parent and live a full and meaningful life.

ELEVEN

Dealing with Confusion and Memory Loss

Older people can exhibit signs of confused thinking for a variety of reasons. They may not be getting enough sleep. They may have taken too much medication. They may not be eating properly. And, in an overwhelming number of cases among the elderly, they may be depressed and anxious. Their unfocused conversation, sense of confusion, disorientation, and inappropriate reactions all can be due to very real physical and emotional problems.

Before we label Mom and Dad "senile," we need to look closely at some possible reasons for their actions.

1) *Are they getting enough sleep?* As we get older, we get less and less deep, restorative sleep. We wake more during the night and sleep more lightly. All of us sometimes awaken feeling as if we haven't slept enough. That's likely to happen more often with elderly people. It often takes them longer to get going in the morning, and they may nap a lot during the day so that it's harder to get to sleep at night. All of this contributes to a feeling of being a beat or two "off"—slightly out of focus. When your mother or father complains of sleepless and restless nights, suggest they try to stay up later and only go to bed when they're really tired. You may have to play detective and question them about sleeping habits. If they're normally close-mouthed, they may not want to trouble you with tales of walk-

ing the floors all night. Chronic poor sleeping should be discussed with your parent's doctor.

2) *Malnutrition.* This is the "tea and toast" syndrome so common-ly associated with older people who live alone or who care for an ailing spouse.

Typically the caretaker half of an elderly couple is so involved in cooking proper meals for a sick spouse and seeing to his medication, exercise, and doctor appointments that she neglects her own wel-fare. The results of her malnutrition are dramatically evident when she falls ill and enters the hospital. At Pendelton Memorial Methodist Hospital in New Orleans, Dr. Albert Barrocas, surgeon and nutrition-support director, says, "Some form of malnutrition is detectable in ap-proximately 50 percent of hospitalized patients."

Many of these elderly people have gradually lost the desire to eat balanced meals. Sometimes their medication robs their appetite. Of-ten they are simply too fatigued and dispirited to bother cooking for themselves and will "grab something" for dinner. They may have un-attended dental problems that prevent them from chewing—miss-ing teeth, poor alignment of remaining teeth, ill-fitting bridges. And there's another, often overlooked reason why older people don't eat well: good food is expensive. When the older person on a fixed in-come sees his grocery bill mounting each month, he may start cut-ting corners.

You know that light-headed, slightly "off" feeling that you get when you've had coffee and juice for breakfast and skipped lunch al-together? Around 3:00 P.M. you feel your concentration slipping, and you don't really care if you finish that report or not. You're robbing your body of "brain food"—the nutrients you need to nourish all your cells, including your brain cells, are missing. You can imagine the effects of long-term, protein-poor eating on an older person.

Signs of Malnutrition—What to Look For and How to Help

The following symptoms often signal malnutrition:

- Sudden weight loss.
- Noticeable slowdown in activity—lethargy, disinterest, chronic fatigue.

- Thinning hair and brittle nails.
- Sores around the inside or outside of the mouth and a burning tongue.
- Puffiness around the ankles.

These can all be signs of vitamin and mineral deficiencies. There are a number of steps you can take to head-off worsening problems:

1) Bring nourishing "CARE" packages. When you make a beef stew or vegetable soup, make some extra for your parents.

2) Check your local telephone directory or call one or two hospitals to find a Meals on Wheels or similar hot-meal program in your area. Meals on Wheels volunteers deliver a nutritious hot meal right to the house five days a week. Discuss the idea with your parents. They'll fight you at first, but when you point out that the doctor suspects they're malnourished and that they show signs of needing hospitalization, they'll choose the lesser of two evils.

3) Take over the grocery shopping. When you notice Dad is living on cottage cheese and crackers in an effort to economize, you can supply him with the foods he needs by "supplementing." One daughter who suspected her father was malnourished offered to do his weekly shopping, to which she added several steaks, chicken breasts, frozen vegetables, and the like from her own freezer. When he demanded to see the receipt so he could pay for the groceries, she showed it to him without qualms. She says, "I knew Dad would construe whatever I did as 'charity' and there'd be hard feelings. This way, he pays for the groceries, and I sneak in good foods he really needs. I always tell him, 'Dad, chicken was very cheap this week at the market, so I put it in the order.' My father has difficulty reading the itemized part of the grocery bill, so I circle the total for him. It's entirely possible that he's onto my little game. And even if he is, so what? He's getting the food he needs, and I sleep a little better at night."

How to Deal with Your Parent's Medication

A little medicine can go a long way for the elderly. Drugs stay in the body longer and can build up in tissues, so doctors are cautious about the amounts of medicine they prescribe for an elderly person. If an older person has trouble remembering whether or not he took his pills and takes one or two extra each day to "play safe," he can begin exhibiting extreme reactions, ranging from lapses into unconsciousness to confusion to uncontrollable agitation.

There are a number of methods open to you for coping with the situation:

1) Call the doctor and find out the side effects of Mom's medicine. It could be that her slurred speech and disorientation are due to an overdose of medication. Also, Mom may be taking conflicting medications prescribed by different doctors. It's imperative that you discuss this with her internist. The pills could be interacting in harmful ways. For your own information, get a copy of the *Physician's Desk Reference*. This book lists possible side effects from medication. The child of an aging parent would do well to refer to it each time Mom is given a new medication.

2) Check the dates on prescription bottles. If she just filled the order three days ago for her one-dose-a-day diabetes medication and ten pills are missing from the bottle, you know she's not following directions.

3) Try one of those new pill counters with compartments for each day's medication. They help Mom keep track not only of her daily dosage but also of today's date—a good memory jogger.

4) If your parent is simply no longer capable of keeping track of her medication, you'll have to arrange for a neighbor or perhaps a nursing student at a nearby hospital to drop by to give her the correct dosage. Or you can arrange with Mom's doctor to order a home health aide or visiting nurse. There are private, for-profit services that send out semi-skilled and skilled personnel to homebound, disabled, and elderly people. If your mother is on insulin and is having trouble remembering whether or not she has had her daily injection, this kind of service can be invaluable. In today's world, most of us cannot manage medication supervision unless our parent lives with us or just a few blocks away.

5) Some of the symptoms of changed behavior you notice could be due to medication. Remember, if Dad has stopped taking his pills

simply because he has forgotten how many to take and when, he could have a reaction to the abrupt cessation of medication. Many people exhibit a variety of withdrawal symptoms, ranging from dizziness to what looks like flu.

6) Keep in mind that older people do not metabolize as quickly as younger folks. Drugs stay in the body longer, so there may be symptoms for several days after your parent has stopped taking a particular medication.

How to Talk to Your Parent's Doctor

It's imperative to feel comfortable about discussing your parent's condition with his doctor. If the doctor treats you like an interloper and refuses to discuss other than strictly medical information, you have two possible courses of action: 1) shop around for a new doctor who is willing to treat the whole person and consider your parent's emotional and social problems as part of his total medical management; or 2) get across to Dad's doctor that you are not an adversary—you want to work with him as a team to help your parent.

You have the right to ask questions. You have the right to be given a rationale for a course of treatment. Many elderly people think of an M.D. as an entity only slightly lower than God. They're intimidated by their doctor. The doctor may have grown used to total acquiescence from your Mom or Dad. When you enter the picture and begin to ask questions, it's a new ball game. Once you tell the doctor that you'll be involved in his patient's treatment, he or she should be willing to work with you.

Be particularly involved when your parent is hospitalized. Mistakes happen in hospitals. If your parent is given an injection, find out what it is. It's not unheard of for bed #2 to get a shot or a pill ordered for bed #1. Keep a watchful eye on treatment, carefully inform the head nurse of any allergies your parent has, and let the hospital staff know you're responsible for Mother or Father's care. Older people who cannot defend themselves and speak up, who often are so disoriented by hospitalization that they don't know what's happening, need an advocate. That's you.

Physical illnesses can also cause confusion. The onset of many geriatric diseases produces symptoms that are not always obvious, particularly if we see our parent frequently. Sometimes, the changes are so gradual that we aren't even aware of when they started. One 60-year-old son's eyes were opened when his cousin came to town for a family wedding. He said, "George noticed that Dad's almost shuffling when he walks now. Dad was always kind of a deliberate, slow mover, so I didn't actually notice the change. George also point-ed out that my father is cranky now, petulant and irritable most of the time. I guess I've just been putting it down to old age. But I'm planning to have a talk with his doctor today."

Much of what we ascribe to old age-stubbornness, lack of con-centration, slipshod grooming—can be due to real physical condi-tions. We have to be alert to the changes.

Physical Changes to Notice

Hearing impairment is common among seniors. When an older per-son cannot hear everything that's said, he becomes frustrated, some-times angry that people aren't talking loudly enough, and, finally, depressed. Watch your parent when you're conversing. If he's not re-sponding directly to your remarks, it could be that he simply can't hear you.

When you broach the subject of hearing, be diplomatic but di-rect. "Dad, you're missing a lot of pleasure in life because you're not hearing as well as you once did. Let's find out about a hearing aid. You'll be able to enjoy the movies again and can take one of those courses at the college." People often resist wearing a hearing aid be-cause they associate it with weakness and old age. They're afraid of being laughed at. So you may not convince him. You can point out the advantages, do some research on hearing aids to give you both a realistic idea of how much they can and cannot help, and mention it from time to time. If Dad does decide to try a hearing aid, chances are he'll feel and act less withdrawn and depressed.

Your parent may be concealing the fact that he falls. If you see bruises or an adhesive bandage placed here and there, chances are he's losing his balance and falling.

Check first to see if he needs stronger glasses. His eyesight may have weakened dramatically. Also, try to encourage him to wear his glasses if he needs them. When an older person with diminished eyesight can't be bothered to wear glasses, he's in danger of tripping over a pair of shoes on the floor or not seeing the curb of the sidewalk.

Dizziness and frequent falling can be another sign of malnutrition. The dizzy, weak person might simply be forgetting to eat. Or that light-headed feeling can be a sign of problems with blood pressure. When your parent stands up from his chair, he may black out and pitch forward because his blood pressure isn't rising quickly enough. Whatever the underlying cause, dizziness and falling must be investigated.

Causes of Confusion: Is It Dementia or Depression?

Dementia is the loss of mental abilities. The older person becomes forgetful to the point that it interferes with daily living. She may not remember whether or not she ate breakfast, turned off the stove, etc. Before the doctor diagnoses dementia, he first checks for other physical causes of the confusion: thyroid conditions, poor nutrition, drug reactions, and the like.

Depression is a disorder of mood. It's accompanied by sadness, pessimistic thinking, a loss of interest in life. Often the depressed person can't be bothered to eat and moves very slowly. Sometimes a depressed individual of any age is so "down" that he wants to stay in bed all the time.

Depression can masquerade as senility. The depressed older person loses interest in food, often abandons life-long grooming habits and becomes slovenly and careless, and turns away from others, even refusing to answer the door or the telephone. By not eating, taking his medicine, or caring for himself, he becomes weaker and more prone to non-logical thinking, which sends him further into the depressive spiral. That's why so many older people who have genuine depression are thought of as senile. A 20-year-old who exhibits those same symptoms is never regarded as senile, although he clearly looks depressed to his family and friends. In an elderly person, it's more difficult to distinguish a psychological depression from signs of early brain degeneration.

Depression is common in older patients who have been sick for several years. The person with a long-term debilitating chronic illness like heart disease or emphysema frequently becomes depressed. This kind of depression is a form of giving up, discouragement, a loss of interest in others, and a social withdrawal. Some of the signs are: poor sleep, pessimistic outlook, sour disposition, and feelings of helplessness and hopelessness. He or she might really feel, "What's the use? I have no bright future to anticipate." The person has no appetite and loses a large amount of weight. Combined with the dehydration brought about by not eating enough, the result is malnutrition. And thus the vicious circle. Mom is depressed, she can't eat, and each day she gets weaker, thus leading to even more depression because she has no energy to deal with daily life.

The bright spot in this scenario is that there is a whole family of new medications for depression that are well tolerated by elderly people, even those on a great deal of other medication.

Anxiety in the Elderly

Older healthy people living alone usually get along well as long as nothing happens to impair their abilities or their self-confidence. But when their situation changes it becomes harder for them to deal with all the daily tasks of living alone. They begin to feel inept. For the person who has been independent his whole life, this sense of "I can't do it anymore" is soul-destroying. People who are by nature sociable and outgoing will tend to ask their family for more and more help. They will naturally turn to the outside world for help with grappling with tasks. If they tend to be solitary, they will withdraw more and more.

Irene Morris had lived alone a long time, ever since her husband died in his early sixties. She had made an excellent adjustment to widowhood and kept busy. She was one of the friendliest people in the high-rise building and managed to go to religious services "religiously." Another important lifeline to the outside world was the daily call she received from her daughter Elizabeth. Liz Morris was a hard-working career banker and desperately needed a vacation. She made her plans for a trip to Europe and explained to her mother that she would not be calling every day as usual.

Irene accepted this and made no comment. It was important to Irene that she not displease or trouble her wonderful, caring daughter. But the first day after Liz left the country, her mother began to worry, to imagine all sorts of dangers inherent in the trip. She kept thinking of the worst case scenarios and eventually found she could not sleep at night and was extremely short of breath. In a panic she called her doctor in the middle of the night and ended up in the local hospital emergency room, being treated for what she was sure was a massive heart attack. Fortunately, her doctor and the emergency staff recognized that Irene was having a panic attack. She simply couldn't deal with her daughter's absence, the disruption of her normal routine.

If your parent has stopped going out of the house, avoids social encounters, calls you several times a day—you should suspect anxiety. Anxiety can sometimes lead to agoraphobia, in which a person will not go out of the house alone or not go out at all. Some people with anxiety limit their range of activities. They may only go to the drugstore or only to the local grocery store, and they may always take the same route. What looks like peculiar "senile" behavior may be a full-blown case of anxiety, and the person may suffer a great deal from it.

Anxiety, like depression, can also be helped by medication. Medicine combined with establishing social contacts for your parent can alleviate their fears in a relatively short time. When Dad gets involved at the local Senior Center or even if he just has periodic visits from a cheerful care-giver, his anxiety level will decrease. He will be able to take a deep breath because he will feel safe.

What should you do if your parent exhibits signs of anxiety or confusion? First, get a full diagnostic workup at a medical center that specializes in geriatric medical management. Make sure your parent is seen by a psychiatrist whose medical training will enable him or her to distinguish between the normal wear and tear of many years, anxiety, depression or actual brain disorder.

What if your parent is suffering from a psychiatric disorder? Psychiatrists who specialize in dealing with geriatric patients dispel the myth that older people are unresponsive to psychiatric treatment. It is estimated that 15 percent of the population over the age of 65 suffers from psychiatric disorders. About half of these people have brain function disorders. With our increased knowledge about brain functioning and a new attitude toward the aging process, more and more older people are being helped.

For some, aging means "letting their hair down" or "letting it all hang out"—in other words, giving themselves permission to act up. Before we dismiss Mom or Dad's unusual behavior as a symptom of a serious brain disorder or decide that "Dad's getting peculiar in his old age,"a diagnostic workup is imperative.

If it's determined that your parent has early signs of dementia, what does this mean and how will it affect your family life?

How Do I Know If It's Alzheimer's?

Alzheimer's disease is a specific type of dementia, one that has received a great deal of publicity. It is, indeed, a devastating, irreversible disease. But many older people with dementia do not have Alzheimer's. Since Alzheimer's is a particular disease with enormous complications, we will not attempt to cover it in this book. There are many excellent books on the subject, and the Alzheimer's Disease and Related Disorders Association (ADRDA) can direct you to books, support programs, and help such as day care centers. Write to them at:

Alzheimer's Disease and Related Disorders Association
4709 Golf Road
Suite 1015
Skokie, IL 60076
Toll-free Help Line: 888-301-1819

There are many other causes of dementia, or reduced mental activity, among the elderly. An older person may have suffered several small strokes that leave no obvious sign, such as facial paralysis, but nevertheless have affected brain cells. Chronic alcoholism is another cause of central nervous system impairment. Certain organophosphates, such as PCBs, if ingested in large quantities can harm brain tissue. And many diseases that affect the central nervous system, such as multiple sclerosis, syphillis, lupus, and others, can bring about forms of dementia.

Geriatric specialists use a wide variety of techniques to help with the first symptom of dementia—persistent memory loss. As adult children of aging parents, we can adapt some of those common-sense methods to help improve the quality of our parents' lives.

Ways to Improve Memory

When we have problems with our memory, we're not *registering* properly. As we age, we remember the name of the boy in school who threw snowballs at us, but the new telephone number we just learned seems to "fly out the window" of our brains. We register information at a different rate as we age. Older people need more time to register what they've just learned. But by establishing certain habits, the new information can get "planted," or "impressed," in the mind. Consider the analogy of how you learned to spell. You were drilled over and over until the repetition registered the word. You had a visual memory of the word so that when you spelled C-A-T, you saw the word written out in your mind. And you further reinforced that image through "muscle memory," repeatedly writing the word "cat."

As we said, it takes the older person longer to register information. But we can help by using some of the following methods that improve memory:

1) *Keep the conversation simple, direct, and to the point.* Don't introduce a lot of extraneous detail. If you want Mom to remember you've taken her towels home to wash, don't go into a long dissertation on whether you'll use hot water, bleach, permanent press cycle, or the like. Just keep repeating that you are washing the towels and will return with them on Saturday.

2) *Reinforce.* Buy Mom a giant-sized calendar, tie a ball point pen to it, and have her write in for Saturday, "Jean is coming here with towels." Writing down, for older people as well as for all of us, serves to reinforce what we're trying to get the mind to register.

3) *Use the power of the written word.* When Mom is aware that her memory is failing, offer to be her "secretary." She'll feel secure knowing that you have a list of important phone numbers and things such as her checking account number. Meanwhile, keep your name and address on a pad near her telephone, anchored to her re-

frigerator by a kitchen magnet, and on a list for *all* her purses. Also make sure the doctor's number as well as "911" is always nearby.

4) *When your parent's memory begins to fail, it's imperative that you assist in paying the bills.*And it's also time for you to look through the check register to be sure she's not giving away money. The elderly often respond to every plea for a donation as if the mass-mailed letter were a personal appeal. A long-time supporter of charities wants to continue the pattern. It's part of her view of herself and contributes to her self-esteem. But you can intervene when Mom is sending $25 to every obscure charity in the universe. Strike a bargain with her, whereby she continues to support her "favorites" and you dump the rest of the requests in the wastebasket. You can assure her with, "You gave plenty of help over the years. Now it's up to the younger people coming along to support those good causes."

5) *Using "triggers" to jolt the memory.* People with cognitive losses have trouble with *immediate recall.*They usually can remember things that happened a long time ago because those events and associations *registered* in their minds. You can teach Mom to use triggers to remind herself. If she's having trouble remembering whether she called to make a dental appointment, encourage her to make a daily list. When she sees "Make Dental Appointment" on today's list, she can get in the habit of checking the item off after she makes the call. Then, if she forgets whether or not she called, she can check her list. The more she learns to reinforce by writing down and then using those written words to trigger her memory, the better she will retain.

6) *Encourage her to concentrate.* Older people, even those with no appreciable brain problems, have difficulty trying to think of or do two things at once. They must focus and concentrate on one task at a time. Teach her not to allow herself to become distracted. Often, it's helpful to encourage her to take up the knitting or crochet work she did in her youth. Counting the stitches is a useful way to force concentration. Knitters of all ages know that to answer a telephone while counting stitches is disastrous.

Normally, we can handle both "executive functions" and "service functions" at the same time. That is, we can plan a menu or organize a work plan while we walk, jog, ride a bicycle, swim, or drive a car. The older person may have to separate the two functions. If he's on the way to the doctor, he may have to concentrate on that task alone: where is the office; what street does he turn on; where is the elevator in relation to the building's entrance; what floor is the office on; and the doctor's name. If he tries to get too fancy and use his "executive function" to think simultaneously about a movie he wants to see, his "service function," getting his feet to take him to the doctor could walk him right past the building.

To understand the analogy a bit better, watch a 30-year-old mother as she disciplines one child, feeds a baby, admonishes another child, sorts laundry, and talks on the telephone at the same time. Her body does everything her mind tells it to do—and all at once. The 80-year-old woman must select what is important and then concentrate only on that.

When we try to help a parent with memory loss, we run the risk of their resenting what they view as interference. It's hard to admit that one's mental powers are going. Many older people attribute their increasing fuzziness of thinking to "having a bad week." When we suggest using some of the above memory aids, they're hurt and angry. If they're firmly entrenched in denying the obvious, talk to their doctor. He can suggest the same things you would, but they're much more likely to accept the ideas from an expert.

Caring for a parent with memory loss can be a demanding, frustrating job. In Chapter 8, we talked about seeking help from friends and other family members as well as community resources. When you use those sources of social and emotional support and don't try to handle it alone, your job can also be a rewarding one, a chance to give back to your parent the love and care he once gave you and now needs himself.

TWELVE

What Does the Future Hold for America's Seniors?

We've seen that the problems facing our aging parents and, con-sequently, us, don't go away. The majority of us are affected by our parents' physical, emotional, and economic losses.

What will happen in ten or twenty years? What will happen when it's our turn to be elderly? Will society care? Will society ad-dress our needs more efficiently than it addresses the needs of our parents' generation? And will our own children care for us as we care for our parents?

America is "graying" at a rapid rate, so that by the year 2030, it's estimated that 20 percent of the population will be 65 or over. Not only will there be more elderly people but because of medical ad-vances, the elderly will live longer. It is likely that these men and women will become a strong political bloc. They will have learned how to exercise political muscle. Even now, older people are a politi-cal and social power group. The 34.5 million members of AARP (American Association of Retired Persons) are making their voices heard in the areas of mandatory retirement, medical and hospital benefits, and the demand for better retirement housing.

With a growing number of seniors, more attention will be paid to their specific problems. Just as we marshaled our efforts behind wip-ing out polio and other devastating childhood diseases during the "baby boom" of the 1950s, we'll step up research on diseases of the elderly—notably, Alzheimer's, arthritis, and osteoporosis. In the last fifteen years we have seen the practice of geriatrics become an important medical specialty. Doctors today simply know more about the aging process and how to "age gracefully." There is an amplified understanding of the role nutrition and exercise play in entering those "golden years." And, most importantly, there has been a definite shift in attitudes toward the older population. As we all face the inevitable, the attitude now is not one of resignation but of problem-solving.

Lawrence Lazarus, M.D., Assistant Professor of Psychiatry at Rush Medical College in Chicago, assistant attending physician at Rush-Presbyterian-St. Luke's Medical Center, and psychiatric consultant to the Johnston R. Bowman Health Center for the Elderly, is hopeful about the future of the elderly in America. He feels that there's likely to be "an increased interest in the aging process with increased societal concern and positive feelings toward our older population."

Dr. Lazarus touches on another future trend. "Middle-aged men with aging parents will play a more active role. The feminist movement has taught men to be more sensitive, to develop the nurturing part of themselves." He points out how young fathers today, for a variety of reasons including the fact that many of their wives are holding down jobs, share responsibility for child-rearing. They fully expect to respond to their children's needs with emotional as well as physical care-giving. Dr. Lazarus sees a rise in what some sociologists call "filial maturity"—the desire by both middle-aged men and women to respond to their parents' needs. He says, "We get a sense of satisfaction from helping our parents, who helped us when we needed them." All of this bodes well for all of us when we grow older!

With changing societal attitudes, new social institutions will spring up to care for an aging population. Just as alternative schools, community youth programs, drug-free residential schools, and adolescent therapy groups arose to handle the "difficult" teen-agers of the sixties and seventies, we'll see innovative programs for older people. It's likely that communes of a different kind may come back into style. Older people may decide that it's easier, more economical, and more fun to live in a group environment rather than living alone in high-rise buildings.

In our era of self-expression, older people have already discovered that being quiet and waiting for one's "just due" doesn't work. When they were young in the 1930s, attention was first paid to the need for a pension for those over 65. As a result, the Federal Insurance Contributory Act (FICA), under which Social Security was the main feature, was passed in 1935 and implemented in 1937. Most workers 65 and up were guaranteed a pension. Contributions were made during working years by both employees and their firms. For the first time in U.S. history retired workers, those who had labored their whole lives, got something more than a gold watch and a handshake.

Then, several years ago along came the ebullient Maggie Kuhn and the Gray Panthers, one of the seniors' first advocacy groups. The Gray Panthers provided us with a model. They've proved that it's productive to band together and make noise about age discrimination. They taught us that it's okay to be old and outrageous. They taught us that they've earned the right to demand what they need— and to keep demanding their rights. When it's our turn to be old, we'll remember those lessons and use them to our advantage.

The need for residential facilities in safe neighborhoods with good access to shops and transportation will continue to grow. And the need for alternatives to nursing homes is now being met and will be met to a greater degree as the population ages. Only a small number of people actually need the skilled care provided by a nursing home. Most older people can benefit from living in a group situation in which they maintain a large measure of independence yet have the security and convenience of helping hands when they're needed.

Group living will become more socially acceptable. People will band together on the basis of special interests. Even now, one group of women writers is scouting for a big old home that can house them when they can no longer live alone. Most of them are happily married and expect to stay so, but they also know that most elderly women in America end up as widows, living on their own. One of the writers, who's now in her early forties, says, "At that point in my life, I'll want a support group. And this bunch will certainly have lively conversations!"

As more people opt for community living, it will become "trendy." Advertising and public relations people will devote their efforts to selling the image. And just as we've come to accept DINCs (double income, no children couples), working mothers, day care centers, and other social phenomena of our era, the group retirement facility will become a commonly accepted way of life. Retirement homes will lose the stigma of "warehouses of the old." Growing old in America will not be the lonely, isolated, frightening experience it is for so many people today.

In this century we've seen the breakdown of many barriers. Values change. Old fears and prejudices wash away. We learn to accept what was not previously accepted, to respect what was denigrated, to appreciate what was ignored. We've proven that we can "walk in another's moccasins." We can reach out to each other—not on the basis of skin color, gender, disability, or surname. Now and in the future, we will learn to deal with "ageism"—and bring down the barriers against seniors.

Appendix of Resources

et's start with governmental agencies on all levels: national, state, and local. In 1965 the U.S. Congress passed the Older Americans Act. This act mandated the establishment of the Administration on Aging, which became part of the Department of Health, Education, and Welfare, more commonly known as HEW. The name has been changed to Department of Health and Human Services, but programs for older Americans are still administered under its auspices.

National programs are carried out in each state. Your state has an Area Agency on Aging office within its Department of Health and Human Services, or a similarly named department. You can learn about its programs and services by consulting the blue pages of your city or town's telephone directory.

Look for the listing "United States Government Offices" and then find the subhead "Health and Human Services, Department of."

For information on specific state programs, look for "State Government Offices." Under that, you'll see listings for individual programs:"Home Care,""Housing," and the like.

If you live in a city or large town, check the blue pages for "City Government Offices" and then subheads on individual services, such as "Aging" or "Human Resources."

When your parent becomes frail and ill, initially, you may feel overwhelmed. Remember, there are many support systems out there. It's a question of locating what you need and finding it as close to home as possible. It's a good idea to contact your local Family Service Agency to help you get started. Many agencies offer counseling as well as suggestions on home care, day care, and nursing homes. A helpful place to start is:

> Alliance for Children and Families
> 11700 W. Lake Park Drive
> Milwaukee, WI 53224
> 414-359-1040

Don't suffer alone! There are self-help groups that can help you.

Children of Aging Parents (CAPS) is a self-help group organized in Levittown, Pennsylvania, almost twenty years ago. This non-profit has grown to fit the national need for support and guidance. They are now a national referral and resource for information on all aspects of care-giving. They publish a national newsletter and can guide you in finding existing support groups in your community as well as help you start your own group. Write:

> CAPS Office
> 1609 Woodburne Road
> Suite 302A
> Levittown, PA 19057
> 215-945-6900
> Website: www.CAPS4caregivers.org

When your parent is diagnosed as having problems with brain function (Alzheimer's disease, dementia, etc.) start by contacting the national office of the Alzheimer's Disease and Related Disorders Association. They function as a clearing house, with information on support groups, day care, home help, and more. You can write to them at:

> Alzheimer's Disease and Related
>   Disorders Association
> 4709 Golf Road
> Suite 1015
> Skokie, IL 60076
> 847-933-1000 greater Chicagoland area
> 888-301-1819 toll-free across the United States

Another excellent source for the myriad problems associated with cognitive losses in the elderly is:

The National Council on Aging
409 Third Street S.W.
Suite 200
Washington, DC 20024
Website: www.ncoa.org

We've already discussed the advocacy groups for the elderly that are growing in power and prestige. Following are two of these organizations:

American Association of Retired Persons
1909 K Street N.W.
Suite 200
Washington, DC 20049

Older Women's League National Office
1325 G Street N.W.
Lower Level B
Washington, DC 20005

Other organizations that can provide you with information on available resources in your community are:

American Society on Aging
833 Market Street
Suite 516
San Francisco, CA 94103
415-974-9600

The ASA specializes in watchdog activities for legislation and programs that affect the elderly population and is also involved in life-long learning programs for senior people. They recently established a Training Center on Aging, in which low-cost leadership training for the elderly is emphasized. They publish a bimonthly newsletter, "Aging Connection," that keeps members up to date on trends and policies.

Center for the Study on Aging
706 Madison Avenue
Albany, NY 12208
518-465-6927

The Center is an excellent source for books and cassette tapes for care-givers, covering such topics as mental health, illness, nutrition, fitness, and rehabilitation.

The National Caucus & Center
    on Black Aged
1424 K Street N.W.
Suite 500
Washington, DC 20005
202-637-8400

The Caucus represents local groups throughout the country and is concerned with all issues that affect black senior citizens. Some of their activities include lobbying for improvement in our laws and owning and managing good rental housing for the black elderly.

As we pointed out in this book, there are many outstanding volunteer programs organized by the federal government and administered on the local level. To learn more about the Foster Grandparents for Children with Special Needs, Senior Companion Program, Retired Senior Volunteer Program, and other volunteer projects, some of which carry a small stipend, call this toll-free number: 800-424-8867.

When your parent needs help, either in his home or yours, you can check locally with your doctor, hospital, and social service agency. In addition, the growing number of professional care managers on our national scene will work to your advantage. Word-of-mouth is often your best guide to locating a skilled care manager who can guide you in the right direction.

When your parent needs a nursing home, contact your local branch of the American Association of Retired Persons, your state government commission that oversees housing for the elderly, your state mental health department, and the gerontology department of your nearby medical center. Collateral reading material will help you and your parent make an informed decision.

When you need a trained third party to help you and your parent form a better relationship, write to:

> American Psychiatric Association
> 400 K Street N.W.
> Washington, DC 20005
>
> The American Psychological Association
> 750 First Street N.E.
> Washington, DC 20002
>
> The National Association of Social Workers
> 750 First Street N.E.
> Washington, DC 20002

BIBLIOGRAPHY

Adler, Alfred, *What Life Should Mean to You*, edited by Alan Porter (New York: Putnam, 1958).

American Association of Retired Persons, *Andrus Foundation Bringing Research to Life*, Washington, DC, 1998

Atkinson, Holly, M.D., *Women and Fatigue* (New York: Putnam, 1985).

Badgwell, Nancy, Ph.D., "The Hardest Decision," *Modern Maturity*, Dec., 1986.

Ball, Jane, *Caring for an Aging Parent, Have I Done All I Can?* (Buffalo: Prometheus Books, 1968).

Benyo, Richard, and Rhonda Provost, *Feeling Fit in Your 40s: How to Get the Most from the Best Years of Your Life* (New York: Atheneum, 1987).

Bluh, Bonnie, *The "Old" Speak Out* (New York: Horizon Press, 1979).

Carlson, Avis D., *In the Fullness of Time* (Chicago: Regnery, 1977).

Cassel, Christine K., M.D., ed., *The Practical Guide to Aging—What Everyone Needs to Know* (New York: NYU Press, 1999).

Cohen, Donna, and Carl Eisdorfer, *Caring for Your Aging Parents* (New York: Putnam, 1993).

Cohen, Stephen Z., Ph.D., and Bruce Michael Gans, *The Other Generation Gap: The Middle Aged and Their Aging Parents* (Chicago: Follett, 1978).

Davis, Steven Andrew, M.D., *How to Stay Healthy in an Unhealthy World* (New York: William Morrow, 1983).

Dreikurs, Rudolf, M.D., and Vicki Soltz, R.N., *Children: the Challenge* (New York: Hawthorn, Dutton, 1964).

Edinberg, Mark A., Ph.D., *Talking with Your Aging Parents* (Boston: Shambhala Publications, 1987).

Egler, Daniel, "Study of Elderly Reveals Hidden Victims of Abuse," *Chicago Tribune*, Dec. 14, 1987.

Feltin, Marie, M.D., *A Woman's Guide to Good Health After 50* (Glenview, IL: American Association of Retired Per-sons, Scott-Foresman, 1987).

Ferguson, Tom, M.D., *Medical Self-Care: Access to Health Tools* (New York: Simon & Schuster, 1980).

Field, Minna, *The Aged, the Family, and the Community* (New York: Columbia University Press, 1972).

Gottlieb, Daniel, with Edward Claflin, *Family Matters: Healing in the Heart of the Family* (New York, Dutton, 1991).

Guralnick, Elissa S., and Paul M. Levitt, *39 Forever: Living Long and Well* (Longmont, CO: Bookmakers Guild, 1986).

Katona, Cornelius L.E., *Depression in Old Age* (United Kingdom: John Wiley & Sons, 1994).

Knopf, Olga, M.D., *Successful Aging,* (New York: Viking Press, 1975).

Kotulak, Ronald, "New Health Bailout Urged for Elderly," *Chicago Tribune,* Nov. 24, 1986.

Kubler-Ross, Elisabeth, *On Death and Dying,* (New York: Macmillan, 1969).

Lebow, Grace, and Barbara Kane with Irwin Lebow, *Coping with Your Difficult Older Parent: A Guide for Stressed-Out Children* (New York: Avon Books, 1990).

Levin, Nora Jean, *How to Care for Your Parents: A Practical Guide to Eldercare* (New York: W.W. Norton & Company, 1997).

Lieber, Phyllis, Gloria S. Murphy, and Annette Merkur Schwartz, *Grown-up Children, Grown-up Parents* (New York, Carol Publishing Group, 1994).

MacLean, Helene, *Caring for Your Parents—A Sourcebook of Options and Solutions for Both Generations* (Garden City, NY: Doubleday, 1987).

Matteson, Michael T., and John M. Ivancevich, *Managing Job Stress and Health* (New York: Macmillan, 1982).

McLeish, John A.B., *The Ulyssean Adult Creativity in the Middle and Later Years* (New York: McGraw-Hill, 1976).

National Academy on an Aging Society, *Demography Is Not Destiny* (New York: The Commonwealth Fund, 1999).

Naunton, Ena, "Malnutrition May Block a Patient's Exit from the Hospital," *Chicago Tribune,* Nov. 8, 1987.

Nierenberg, Gerard I., and Henry H. Calero, *Meta-Talk* (New York: Trident Press, 1973).

Nirenberg, Jesse S., Ph.D., *Breaking Through to Each Other* (New York: Harper and Row, 1976).

Otten, Alan L., "The New Old," *The Wall Street Journal,* Vol. LXVIII, No. 146.

Psychiatric News, "Treating the Elderly Calls on Different Skills, But Success Is Probable,"Vol. XXII, No. 17 (Sept. 4, 1987).

Rabins, Peter V., M.D., Mary Jane Lucas, R.N., and Nancy L. Mace, M.A., "The Impact of Dementia on the Family," *Journal of the American Medical Association,* Vol. 248, No. 3 (July 16, 1982).

Research and Education Association, *Human Aging* (U.S. Public Health Service, 1982).

Secunda, Victoria, *When You and Your Mother Can't Be Friends* (New York: Bantam Doubleday Dell, 1990).

Sloan, Bernard, *The Best Friend You'll Ever Have* (New York: Crown, 1980).

Statistical Abstract of the United States, 1986, 10th Edition (U.S. Department of Commerce, Bureau of the Census).

Tomb, David A., M.D., *Growing Old: A Complete Guide to the Physical, Emotional and Financial Problems of Aging* (New York: Viking Penguin, 1984).

Wood, John, "Labors of Love," *Modern Maturity,* Aug.–Sept., 1987.

Yates, Ronald E., "Aging in Japan," *Chicago Tribune,* Aug. 7, 1986.

INDEX